Deuteronomy

Dwelling in God's Word

Deuteronomy

Remembering and Renewing the Covenant of Love:
A Fifty-Day Devotional

GRAHAM JOSEPH HILL

Eagna Publishing • Sydney, Australia

DEUTERONOMY
Remembering and Renewing the Covenant of Love: A Fifty-Day Devotional

Published by: Eagna Publishing (Sydney, Australia)
eagnapublishing@icloud.com
Cover and interior design: Graham Joseph Hill
www.grahamjosephhill.com

paperback isbn: 978-1-7644455-1-1
ebook isbn: 978-1-7644455-2-8
version number: 2026-01-01

Contents

Introduction

This devotional is part of a larger pilgrimage through Scripture, shepherded by Rev. Dr. Graham Joseph Hill, as he walks with readers from Genesis to Revelation. The Dwelling in God's Word series (both podcast and written reflections) invites you to discover how each book of the Bible speaks to the deep longings of the soul and the demands of our shared life in the world. It's not merely a reading plan; it's a sacred journey of formation and transformation. Here, the biblical narrative meets everyday discipleship in prayerful and practical ways.

The Book of Deuteronomy stands at the edge of promise. The wilderness lies behind, the Jordan shimmers ahead. A new generation gathers to listen as Moses, the old shepherd-prophet, speaks one last time. His words aren't simply law, they're love remembered, covenant renewed, faith rekindled. Deuteronomy is a book for those standing on thresholds, those who've come far but know the journey of faith is never finished.

Here, memory becomes sacred ground. Moses reminds the people who they are and whose they are. He calls them to remember mercy in their story, to rehearse the faithfulness that carried them through rebellion and desert, hunger and grace. Again and again, he insists: to love God is to live, to obey is to flourish, to remember is to remain free.

This book resounds with tenderness and urgency. Its laws are invitations to love wholeheartedly, to build justly, to worship faithfully, to live as a people shaped by gratitude rather than fear. Through its pages, God's voice is both commanding and compassionate: "Choose life. Remember my goodness. Walk in my ways."

Deuteronomy is the gospel of memory and renewal. It reminds us that every generation must decide again who it'll serve, what story it'll live by, and how it'll embody love in the land it inhabits. Standing on the edge of promise, it calls us to remember grace, to renew covenant, and to step forward with hearts awake to the God who still speaks.

This devotional is rooted in the richness of the biblical text and nourished by careful theological reflection. It invites you to sit with Scripture: slowly, reverently, attentively. Each entry draws you deeper into Deuteronomy, exposing overlooked treasures and summoning fresh faith. But this isn't just about knowing more. It's about living differently. As you journey through these pages, you'll be challenged to embrace justice, embody mercy, cultivate humility, and become a participant in the reconciling mission of God.

These reflections don't avoid hard questions or flatten the text into sentiment. They dare to wrestle. To pray. To imagine. And they call you to more than contemplation. They invite you to action: to live the lessons of Deuteronomy in your neighborhood, your body, your workplace, your church.

As you immerse yourself in this devotional, may your theology deepen, your heart soften, and your hands be ready to serve. May these fifty days in Deuteronomy stir something courageous in you: a longing to see and be seen by the living Christ.

How to Use This Devotional:

1. This book leads you through Deuteronomy in fifty short devotions.

2. You're encouraged to pair this with the companion podcast: https://grahamjosephhill.com/devotions.

3. Each day, you're invited to:

a. Read the passage slowly, letting it read you.

b. Sit with the day's devotion and let its truths sink deep.

c. Pray, honestly and vulnerably, into the text.

d. Discern one concrete action in response.

Whether you read alone, with family, or within a community, this journey through Deuteronomy will shape your heart and stretch your faith. Come ready to be changed.

Day 1: Time to Move Forward

Reading: Deuteronomy 1:1–8

The story opens with Israel camped in the wilderness, staring at a horizon they've seen for far too long. Moses stands before them: old, weathered, and wise. The wilderness has been both punishment and preparation. Forty years earlier, fear had kept their parents from entering the land of promise. Now, a new generation listens as Moses speaks the words of God: "You've stayed long enough at this mountain. Break camp and advance."

The first verses of Deuteronomy are a map of the soul. The mountain they must leave is Horeb, where they first encountered divine presence in thunder and fire. It's where they learned reverence, where law and covenant were born. But even sacred places can become prisons when nostalgia replaces obedience. God tells them it's time to move: not because the mountain is unholy, but because holiness always moves outward.

Spiritually, this passage is about transitions: the call to trust again after failure, to move when it would be easier to stay. Each of us has our Horeb, a season or place where we've met God profoundly. Yet the danger is to build a camp instead of a journey, to confuse past encounter with present calling. The voice of God still speaks: "You've stayed long enough." Growth always involves leaving something good for something greater.

Divine faithfulness is the hinge. God doesn't call Israel into the unknown without promise: "See, I've given you this land." Grace always precedes command. The invitation to "go in and possess" is grounded in what God has already done. Likewise, Jesus assures us that those who ask will receive, those who seek will find. Faith responds to God's blessing.

For our lives today, Deuteronomy 1:1–8 becomes a mirror. Where have we stayed too long, clinging to old certainties, habits, or wounds? Where has fear or comfort replaced trust? God's call isn't just to leave but to advance: to become participants in redemption's story, to live as people of peace and promise. Moving forward means learning to forgive, to serve, to risk loving again, to believe that grace still opens up new lands ahead.

And in Jesus, this call finds its fullness. He's the new Moses leading us from bondage to freedom, from wilderness wandering to the land of grace. He walks ahead, saying, "Follow me," turning every fear-filled threshold into a doorway of trust.

Guiding Truth: When God says, "You've stayed long enough," grace is already waiting in the land ahead, so we can trust God and move forward.

Reflection: Where might I be clinging to the familiar instead of trusting God's invitation to move forward? What would advancing toward God's promise look like in my relationships, vocation, or inner life?

Prayer: Faithful God, give me courage to leave what's comfortable and step toward what's promised. When fear is present, please remind me of your faithfulness. Lead me from stillness to trust, from hesitation to hope, from the mountain of memory into the land of your living grace. Amen.

Day 2: Shared Leadership and the Weight of Justice

Reading: Deuteronomy 1:9–18

As Moses recounts Israel's wilderness journey, he pauses to remember the moment when leadership had to expand. The burden of guiding, judging, and caring for the people had grown too heavy for one person. So, God instructed Moses to appoint wise, understanding, and respected individuals to share the load. "How can I bear your problems, your burdens, and your disputes all by myself?" he asks. The response is a system of justice and discernment rooted not in power but in shared wisdom.

This moment is both deeply practical and profoundly theological. God's people are learning that holiness is communal: that discernment, accountability, and justice belong to all, not just to the few. The Spirit that once burned in a single bush now begins to flicker in a community. The burden of one becomes the calling of many. Israel's identity as a people of covenant will depend on this truth: that leadership is service, and authority is meant to protect, not exploit.

Moses' words also reflect the tension every leader and community face: the limits of strength, the fatigue of responsibility, the temptation to control. Authentic leadership begins with humility, with confessing, "I can't do this alone." God never asked Moses to carry the whole nation; God asked him to trust that wisdom and faithfulness could multiply through others.

Spiritually, this passage speaks to the soul of community and vocation. Whether we lead families, congregations, workplaces, or friendships, none of us is called to carry the weight alone. The life of faith requires shared discernment, mutual care, and courage to entrust others with responsibility. When we hoard control, we choke the Spirit's work. When we share it, justice and compassion flourish. Faith matures when "I" becomes "we." The kingdom of God is sustained not by solitary heroes but by interdependent communities of grace.

This passage also challenges our understanding of justice. Moses tells the appointed judges, "Don't show partiality in judging; hear both small and great alike. Don't be afraid of anyone, for judgment belongs to God." Justice, in the biblical vision, is holy work: a reflection of divine character. It requires courage, patience, and humility. In an age of loud voices and quick judgment, this command calls us back to reverence: to the listening heart that seeks truth without fear or favoritism.

Through Jesus, we see this justice embodied. He carries the burdens of others, listens without bias, restores dignity to the overlooked, and invites us to do the same. Leadership in his kingdom looks like a towel and a basin, not a throne and a sword.

Guiding Truth: God's work is never meant to rest on one person's shoulders: share the burden, seek justice together, and trust wisdom to multiply.

Reflection: Where am I trying to carry alone what God intends to share through community? How can I practice justice and discernment with humility, courage, and compassion?

Prayer: God of wisdom, teach me to lead by serving and to trust your Spirit in others. Free me from control, fear, and pride. Help me seek justice without partiality and share your work with humility and joy. Let our community reflect your justice and love. Amen.

Day 3: Fear at the Threshold

Reading: Deuteronomy 1:19–46

Moses recalls the turning point that changed everything. Israel had come to the edge of promise. From Horeb to Kadesh-barnea, the journey was swift and full of hope. God had said, "See, I've set the land before you; go up and take possession." But standing at the threshold, fear took hold. The people sent spies to scout the land. The report returned full of both fruit and giants, milk and dread. And instead of remembering deliverance, they remembered fear. They refused to go forward.

This passage is one of Scripture's most tragic memories: not because of divine wrath, but because of wasted possibility. The generation that saw seas split and manna fall couldn't imagine a future secured by faith rather than sight. Moses pleads with them: "Don't be terrified; don't be afraid of them. The Lord your God, who goes before you, will fight for you." But they couldn't hear it. Fear drowned out faith. Trust withered beneath anxiety. The wilderness, meant as passage, became home.

Spiritually, this story exposes a pattern that lives in every human heart. Fear often arises when freedom is near. The closer we come to promise, the louder our anxieties shout. Fear masquerades as wisdom, demanding more proof before obedience. But the voice of God rarely waits for certainty; it calls for trust in uncertainty. We, too, stand at thresholds (new seasons, risks, callings) and face the same temptation to retreat into safety. The tragedy of Kadesh isn't their lack of power; it's their lack of trust.

Fear says, "What if God doesn't answer?" Faith says, "God is good, even if I can't see the answer yet." The disciples' prayer ("Your kingdom come") is the opposite of Kadesh. It's surrender in motion, a willingness to move toward divine purposes even when the terrain ahead looks impossible.

This passage also redefines failure. Israel's rebellion delayed the promise, but it did not destroy it. God's faithfulness outlasted their fear. Grace waited on the other side of disobedience. Even when they tried to "go up and fight" after being told not to, God remained God: merciful but firm, teaching them that faith can't be manufactured by panic or pride. The only way forward is through humble trust.

In Christ, the story turns again. Where Israel faltered at the border, Jesus stands firm in the wilderness, trusting the Father's word against fear and temptation. His obedience redeems our hesitation. In him, every threshold becomes an altar of trust, every fear an invitation to faith.

Guiding Truth: When fear stands between you and God's promise, remember: the One who calls you forward also goes before you.

Reflection: What "thresholds" in my life am I afraid to cross, even though God's presence is clear? How can prayer reshape my fear into trust, my hesitation into faith-filled action?

Prayer: God of courage and compassion, when fear whispers "turn back," help me remember your faithfulness. Please give me the strength to step forward, not by sight but by trust. Lead me past hesitation into the land of your promise, where love casts out fear and grace goes before me. Amen.

Day 4: The Long Way Around

Reading: Deuteronomy 2:1–25

After the rebellion at Kadesh, Israel turns back toward the wilderness. The text begins with a haunting phrase: "Then we turned and journeyed into the wilderness by the way of the Red Sea, as the Lord had told me." It's the story of a generation circling deserts, learning through delay. God leads them "a long time around Mount Seir." Not because the promise is revoked, but because hearts need re-formation. The wilderness becomes a slow apprenticeship in trust.

As they travel, God's instructions are strangely gentle. "Don't harass or provoke Edom, Moab, or Ammon," the people are told. These neighboring nations, descended from Esau and Lot, aren't enemies but kin. Their land isn't for Israel to take, for God has given it to them. Israel's task isn't conquest but respect: to move through without greed or aggression, to buy food and water, to honor boundaries. In this detour, God is teaching them something new: faith isn't only about where you're going; it's about how you travel.

Spiritually, this passage speaks to seasons of delay and detour. We all know what it means to walk in circles, waiting for promises that seem to hover just out of reach. Yet these are the places where God reshapes the soul: where patience, humility, and peace become deeper than victory. The long way is often mercy disguised. In the detour, God weans us from entitlement, teaching us to see others not as obstacles but as fellow recipients of grace.

Moses reminds the people that even in these wanderings, God sustained them: "The Lord your God has blessed you in all the work of your hands. You have lacked nothing." What a strange mercy, to walk nowhere fast and still be fed every day. The wilderness is proof that divine provision isn't dependent on progress. We're sustained not because we've arrived, but because God is faithful. The God of Exodus and Deuteronomy is the same God Jesus reveals: a provider who walks beside us, not a taskmaster waiting at the finish line.

Then comes the turning point in verse 24: "Rise up, set out, and cross the Arnon Valley." After years of circling, the command comes again: go forward. The long detour was never the end, only preparation. In the same way, Christ calls us through our long seasons of waiting into new courage and generosity. We move forward not with arrogance, but with gratitude shaped by grace.

Every long way around prepares us for love: the kind that respects others' inheritance, trusts divine timing, and believes that no journey is wasted in the hands of a faithful God.

Guiding Truth: The long way is never wasted: God uses delay to form humility, deepen trust, and prepare us for promise.

Reflection: What "long way" am I walking right now, and how might God be using it to shape my trust? How can I show peace, patience, and respect for others' paths while waiting for my own promise?

Prayer: Patient God, teach me to trust you in the detours. When the road feels endless, please remind me of your presence and provision. Form in me a spirit of humility and gratitude, that I may walk gently and love faithfully, even on the long way around. Amen.

Day 5: When God Fights for You

Standing again on the edge of promise, Moses recalls two encounters that reveal both divine power and human frailty. First comes King Sihon of Heshbon, who refused Israel's request to pass through his land peacefully. God hardens Sihon's heart, not to destroy him capriciously, but to display sovereignty in a world of human pride. When Sihon attacks, Israel wins a victory it never could have achieved alone. Then comes Og of Bashan, a ruler described in almost mythical proportions, with fortified cities and an iron bed. Yet even this giant of a king falls before the hand of God. These battles mark the transition from wilderness wandering to forward movement. The generation that once feared giants now learns that God goes before them.

At first glance, this passage appears to be about ancient conquest, but its more profound truth lies in how God teaches a hesitant people to trust again. The victories over Sihon and Og aren't about violence for its own sake; they're sacraments of courage, reminders that divine faithfulness still holds. Israel's strength lies not in weaponry or numbers but in the presence of the One who fights for them. They're learning that the real battle is never merely against flesh and blood; it's against despair, unbelief, and the paralyzing weight of fear.

Spiritually, this story speaks to the often-hidden wars within us: the resistance of the heart that refuses to yield, the strongholds of pride or addiction, the fear that God's promises might not be enough. Like Sihon, we sometimes close our hearts to peace. Like Og, we build fortresses to protect what was never ours to defend. Yet the same God who dismantled these empires still works to free us from inner kingdoms of fear and control. The lesson of these victories is about trust: "Don't be afraid of them, for the Lord your God will fight for you."

Faith is surrender to the God who already moves ahead of us. The childlike trust of faith replaces the anxiety of self-reliance. Just as Israel learned to move forward because of divine presence, so we learn to act boldly because the Creator's goodness goes before us.

For followers of Christ, these ancient battles point to the greater victory that has already been won. On the cross, the true King defeats the powers of sin and death: the unseen "Sihons" and "Ogs" that enslave hearts. What we face now aren't conquests but divine callings to live in the freedom of a victory already secured, to walk with courage and compassion in a world still haunted by fear.

Faith today means stepping forward when we feel small, trusting that God's strength is enough for whatever stands ahead. The giants still fall, not by might, but by mercy.

Guiding Truth: When fear looms large, remember God goes before you and that the battle belongs to grace, not to your strength.

Reflection: What "giants" or inner battles am I facing that require trust, not control? How can I practice courageous obedience, confident that God's power and presence precede me?

Prayer: Strong and faithful God, when fear rises and obstacles seem vast, remind me that you go before me. Teach me to trust your strength, not my own. Let my victories be your grace in motion, and my courage a testimony to your unfailing love. Amen.

Day 6: The Gift and the Task

Reading: Deuteronomy 3:12–22

The land east of the Jordan has been conquered. Moses now divides it among the tribes of Reuben, Gad, and the half-tribe of Manasseh. It's fertile land, a place of rest and abundance after decades of dust and wandering. Yet even as these tribes receive their inheritance, Moses reminds them that their freedom isn't complete until all Israel enters into the promise. "You shall cross over armed before your brothers … until the Lord gives rest to your kindred as to you." Their blessing carries responsibility. Rest can't be hoarded; it must be shared.

This passage holds a tension central to the life of faith: the balance between gift and mission. The tribes of the east might have been tempted to settle, to savor their comfort and say, "We've made it." But Moses calls them to remember that covenant life is communal. In God's economy, no one truly rests until everyone does. Grace, when rightly received, always sends us outward.

This is a profound word for those of us living in comfort while others still struggle. We, too, stand on the safe side of a river, called to cross back in solidarity and love. Spiritual maturity isn't measured by how much peace we possess, but by how much peace we pursue for others. The call of these verses is to reject private spirituality and embrace shared vocation: to see our blessings not as private property, but as provision for the work of justice, mercy, and companionship.

At the same time, Moses reassures the people: "Don't be afraid of them, for the Lord your God himself will fight for you." This promise anchors both courage and compassion. Those who cross rivers for the sake of others don't go alone. Divine presence accompanies those who serve, confront, or restore. Fear fades when love drives us beyond self-interest.

Just as the eastern tribes were asked to join their kin in battle, so we're asked to pray and act for the flourishing of others: the hungry, the oppressed, the forgotten. Faith that remains private isn't biblical faith; it's fear in disguise.

Through Christ, this call takes on new depth. He's the One who, though seated in glory, crosses back into our wilderness to lead us home. He doesn't rest until all creation is redeemed. Following him means carrying that same pattern of self-giving love: crossing rivers of fear, comfort, or indifference for the sake of others' freedom.

Faithful presence is always active, generous, and shared. The inheritance we've received in Christ becomes the strength by which we help others find their rest in God.

Guiding Truth: True rest is never private: God blesses us so we can cross back and help others find freedom, too.

Reflection: Where have I settled into comfort while others still wait for freedom, healing, or hope? How might I "cross over" in love: serving, giving, or standing beside others until they share in God's rest?

Prayer: God of justice and mercy, thank you for the land of peace you've given me. Don't let me keep it to myself. Give me courage to cross rivers for others' sake, to fight for their freedom, and to share in your work of love until all find rest in you. Amen.

Day 7: When God Says "No" in Love

Reading: Deuteronomy 3:23–29

Moses prays one of the most vulnerable prayers in Scripture. After years of leading, aching, interceding, and carrying a weary people through the wilderness, he asks God for one more gift: "Let me go over and see the good land beyond the Jordan." It's a simple request from a faithful servant. But the answer comes with unsettling firmness: "That's enough. Don't speak to me of this matter again." Moses will see the land from the mountain's height, but he won't enter it.

This moment is tender and severe. Moses isn't punished here; God holds him. God allows him the beauty of vision but withholds the experience of arrival, not because the promise has failed, but because Moses' part in the story is complete. The mantle will pass to Joshua. The future belongs to another generation. Moses must release what he longed for so God's larger work can unfold.

Spiritually, this passage invites us into the difficult grace of limitation. We all know what it feels like to stand on the edge of a long-held dream and hear a divine "no." Sometimes the "no" arrives as closed doors, unfulfilled hopes, leadership transitions we didn't choose, ministries we must hand over, or seasons we must let go of before they feel finished. In those moments, disappointment feels holy and heavy. The heart protests, "But I've come so far."

Yet Moses teaches us a deeper obedience, the obedience of relinquishment. Faith is trusting God when doors close. The same God who leads us through seas and deserts also leads us into surrender. The "no" isn't rejection. It's realignment. It reminds us that the story isn't ours to control, that the kingdom doesn't rest on our shoulders, and that others will carry the mission forward with a grace we may never fully witness.

This kind of surrender is cruciform worship. It's the posture that frees us from the illusion that our significance depends on finishing everything we start. Moses doesn't sulk or resist. He strengthens Joshua. He blesses the one who'll go further than he can. He lives out a love that's bigger than ego: a love that rejoices when others walk into promises we helped prepare but will never inhabit.

In Jesus, this surrender finds its purest expression. He entrusts the future of his mission to disciples who're still fumbling and fearful. He accepts limitations in his humanity. He lays down life itself. His path shows us that self-giving love is the truest form of leadership. To follow him is to accept that some fruit we plant will bloom in someone else's lifetime, and that this, too, is grace.

Guiding Truth: When God closes a door, trust that the surrender asked of you is part of a larger story grace is still writing.

Reflection: What hope, role, or season might God be inviting me to release so that others can step into their calling? How can I bless, encourage, or strengthen the "Joshua figures" in my life?

Prayer: God of wisdom and tenderness, teach me to trust you in every "no." Loosen my grip on what I cling to, and free my heart to bless those who walk where I can't. Let my surrender become worship, and my release become an offering of love. Amen.

Day 8: The Fire That Forms Us

Reading: Deuteronomy 4:1–24

Moses speaks with the urgency of someone who knows he's delivering his final words. Standing before a generation poised for promise, he says: "Hear the decrees . . . follow them . . . so that you may live." This isn't legalism but love. Moses is telling them that life (true life) flows from listening deeply to God's voice and shaping their days around it.

He reminds them of what they witnessed: the God who brought them out of Egypt with signs and wonders, the God who spoke from fire at Horeb, the God who drew near without consuming them. No other nation had experienced anything like it. The point is clear: Israel's obedience isn't a burden; it's a response to breathtaking grace.

But woven into this tenderness is a warning. Moses knows the human heart drifts. He knows how quickly awe fades and how easily trust turns into forgetfulness. He warns them not to make idols: whether carved from wood, shaped from metal, or formed in imagination. Idolatry isn't just about statues; it's about giving ultimate devotion to what can't save. It's about letting something smaller than God take up the space meant for love, justice, and trust. Moses knows that idols shrink the soul. They take a people formed in divine presence and turn them into anxious consumers, fearful imitators, restless wanderers.

Spiritually, this passage presses on us with the same holy weight. We're shaped by what we adore. Whatever has our attention, loyalty, and longing becomes the fire that forms us. If we cling to approval, success, comfort, or control, those desires will mold us into something smaller than we're meant to be. But when we listen (really listen) to the voice that called us out of our own Egypts, when we let divine love burn away illusions, we become spacious, courageous, and free.

Moses' call isn't simply "Obey the rules." It's "Remember who you are." Remember the grace that rescued you. Remember the One who spoke from fire and lived among you in cloud. Remember the love that carried you when you wanted to return to bondage. Memory becomes the guardrail of faith. Forgetfulness becomes the doorway to idolatry.

For Christians, this entire passage pulls us toward Jesus: the One who embodies the nearness Moses describes. In him, the God who once spoke from fire now speaks in flesh and compassion. In him, we see holiness that doesn't destroy but restores. In him, we find the only One worthy of our worship, the only voice whose commands give life, the only presence strong enough to burn away lesser loves without burning us.

To follow Jesus is to listen again, to let divine love reorder our desires, to reject the idols that promise life but can't give it, and to live with hearts anchored in the presence that has carried us this far.

Guiding Truth: Turn from every lesser love and cling to the God whose presence forms, frees, and fills you with life.

Reflection: What desires or attachments most threaten to become idols in my life, drawing my attention and trust away from God? How can I practice remembering, rehearsing God's faithfulness so my heart stays anchored in truth?

Prayer: Holy One, burn away my idols with the fire of your love. Teach me to listen again, to remember your faithfulness, and to cling to the presence that gives life. Shape my heart in your likeness and lead me into the freedom of wholehearted devotion. Amen.

Day 9: The God Who Finds Us in Exile

Reading: Deuteronomy 4:25–40

Moses looks beyond Israel's immediate future and into a distant horizon filled with both warning and hope. He tells the people that a day will come when they forget the covenant, drift toward idols, and lose themselves among nations not their own. It's a bleak vision. He speaks of scattering, of sorrow, of the slow unraveling that happens when the heart turns from the living God to the smaller gods of desire and fear.

But Moses doesn't end with despair. He says something astonishing for a book so steeped in law: "From there you will seek the Lord your God and you will find God, if you search with all your heart and soul." From there: meaning from the place of loss, exile, regret, confusion. Not from purity or perfection, but from the very places shaped by our wandering.

This passage reveals the rhythm of divine love: judgment that never abandons, discipline that never ceases to pursue, holiness that refuses to turn cold. Moses reminds them of who God really is: the One who speaks from fire, rescues from bondage, creates nations from nothing, and loves with a stubborn, burning fidelity. This God doesn't discard the unfaithful; this God finds them in their ruins.

Spiritually, these verses hit close to home. Many of us know what it's like to feel scattered, internally or externally. We know seasons when our choices deformed us, when our idols took more from us than they ever gave, when life felt exiled from joy or purpose. Moses' words become a lifeline: From there, you can seek God. From there, God will meet you.

This is the gospel before the gospel, the declaration that grace isn't limited by geography, morality, or circumstance. God finds us in our "there," in the middle of what we made, what we lost, or what we can't fix. And God doesn't meet us with scolding, but with mercy. "The Lord your God is a compassionate God," Moses says. Compassion (not anger, not weariness, not abandonment) is the final word.

These verses also teach us how to live with integrity and hope. They call us to humility, honesty, and remembering. We turn away from idols when we name them. We turn toward God when we remember who God has been. This remembrance shapes justice, compassion, and courage. A people who know they've been found can become people who seek the lost. A heart restored to grace becomes a heart that offers grace.

For Christians, this promise shines most brightly in Jesus: the One who comes into every exile we create, who walks into our "there" with healing in hand. He's the God who gathers the scattered, who restores the restless, who speaks mercy in the places where shame once swallowed us whole.

The call is simple and searching: turn, remember, seek. And trust that the One who has always been faithful will be faithful still.

Guiding Truth: Wherever you are (even in exile), turn your heart toward God, and you'll find compassion already moving toward you.

Reflection: What's my "there": the place of spiritual drift, disappointment, or exile where God is inviting me to seek anew? How can remembering God's past faithfulness anchor my heart in hope today?

Prayer: Compassionate God, meet me in my "there." In my scattered places, speak mercy again. Turn my heart toward you, restore what's broken, and lead me back into the freedom of your love. Please make me a witness of grace that finds us even in exile. Amen.

Day 10: Refuge for the Wandering Heart

Reading: Deuteronomy 4:41–49

Before Moses continues his great sermon, the narrative pauses. Three cities of refuge are established east of the Jordan, places where someone who has unintentionally taken a life can run for safety. The timing is striking. Before giving more law, before crossing the Jordan, before Israel receives a single portion of the promised land, God ensures that mercy has an address. Grace is built into the land.

These cities bear witness to a God who knows human frailty. Moses names each city (Bezer, Ramoth, and Golan) and marks them as sanctuaries where justice and compassion meet. No one is beyond the need for refuge, and no one is beyond the reach of it. In a world where vengeance spills easily across generations, God carves out spaces where fear is interrupted and dignity is protected.

This small passage reveals something profound about the character of God. Divine holiness shelters the broken, fallen, and vulnerable, offering them hope. Divine justice is measured, protective, and fiercely compassionate. Before Israel steps into its identity as a people of law, God teaches them that law must serve mercy. Before they learn how to judge, they learn how to protect. A just community is always born from the heart of a compassionate God.

Spiritually, these verses remind us that refuge is a lived reality that every soul needs. Each of us carries moments that haunt us, choices made without malice but with consequences, failures we wish we could undo. God's first impulse doesn't bend toward condemnation but toward sanctuary and even redemption. There's a place to run. There's space to breathe. There's a God who understands our limits and meets us with compassion when life's weight becomes unbearable.

As followers of Christ, we see these cities pointing toward a deeper refuge. Jesus becomes the sanctuary not bounded by geography but by grace. In him, those who are weary, guilty, frightened, or lost find shelter that can't be revoked. He's the place where justice and mercy embrace without contradiction. His presence becomes the refuge for hearts undone by sorrow or shame: the One who welcomes without hesitation and restores without condition.

And if he's our refuge, then we're called to become people of refuge. Our lives (our lands, our homes, our communities, our families, our churches) must be safe places for others who stumble, struggle, or carry burdens too heavy to name. To follow Jesus is to shift from judgment to compassion, from vengeance to understanding, from suspicion to welcome. It's to carry in our character what God established in the land: mercy first. Sanctuary before scrutiny. Safety before sentence.

These few verses, easy to overlook, speak of the shape of a kingdom rooted in compassion and grace. God builds refuge into the very soil so that mercy becomes the foundation of everything else that follows.

Guiding Truth: Let your life become a refuge, mirroring the God who shelters fragile hearts with mercy and wisdom.

Reflection: Where in my life do I need to run toward God's refuge: seeking mercy, rest, or restoration? How can I become a place of sanctuary for others, offering compassion instead of judgment?

Prayer: God of refuge, gather me into your sheltering presence. Meet me where I'm fragile, restore what's bruised, and steady my heart in your mercy. Make my life a sanctuary for others, reflecting your compassion, justice, and unending grace. Amen.

Day 11: The Commands That Shape Us Toward Life

Reading: Deuteronomy 5:1–21

Moses gathers the people and invites them to hear the covenant anew: "The Lord made this covenant with us . . . with all of us who are alive here today." He wants them to know that the Ten Words spoken at Sinai aren't relics of a past generation. They're living speech: holy breath shaping a people into freedom. These commandments aren't shackles; they're the architecture of a life rooted in love, truth, and justice.

Moses reminds them that God didn't whisper from a distance. God spoke "face to face out of the fire": a fierce tenderness, a holy nearness. The commandments come from a God who liberates before asking anything, who rescues before commanding obedience. The great "you shall" and "you shall not" flow from "I'm the Lord your God who brought you out of Egypt." Grace establishes the relationship; obedience sustains it.

These Ten Words teach us what love looks like in motion. Love directed upward: worship without idols, devotion without dilution, reverence without superstition. Love directed inward: rest that heals the exhausted soul, a weekly reminder that we aren't machines but beloved. Love directed outward: honoring parents, protecting life, practicing fidelity, speaking truth, resisting greed, and refusing exploitation. These aren't rules for earning blessings but pathways to flourishing. They order our desires, ground our community, and turn our hearts toward wholeness.

Spiritually, this passage invites examination. Not the grim self-scrutiny that leads to shame, but the kind that awakens desire for deeper freedom. Each command presses gently on the fractures of our lives. Where do I chase idols that promise much but drain my soul? Where do my words wound instead of heal? Where do hidden desires distort my relationships? These questions aren't indictments; they're invitations. God's commands don't crush; they reveal the places where love longs to grow.

These commandments also shape how we live in community. They call us to humility, to truthfulness, to compassion that protects neighbors from harm. The commands to honor life, honor commitments, guard truth, and resist covetousness form a people who refuse to treat others as commodities. They invite us into a society where peace is possible, where dignity is honored, and where injustice finds no foothold.

And in Jesus, these Ten Words become even more radiant. He embodies every command: not as rigid law but as living love. He shows us what it means to love God with heart, soul, and strength, and to love neighbor as ourselves. He deepens the commands, not by burdening us, but by calling us inward: to the desires, motives, and intentions that shape who we are. In him, obedience becomes liberation, not obligation.

These commandments aren't about restriction; they're about becoming fully human: people shaped by divine love, reflecting divine character, walking in divine grace.

Guiding Truth: Let God's commands shape your inner life so that love (real, courageous love) flows through everything you do.

Reflection: Which of these Ten Words is pressing most deeply on my heart right now, inviting change or healing? How might obedience to love (toward God, strangers, enemies, fellow believers, and neighbors) reshape my relationships and choices this week?

Prayer: Holy One, speak your words into my heart again. Let your commands become pathways of freedom, shaping my desires and actions in love. Cleanse what's twisted, heal what's wounded, and form me into someone who reflects your truth, compassion, and grace. Amen.

Day 12: Hearing the Voice That Forms a People

Reading: Deuteronomy 5:22–33

Moses reminds the people of what happened at Sinai: the mountain burning with fire, the thick cloud, the trembling earth, and the voice: pure, overwhelming, unbearably holy. The Ten Words had been spoken aloud by God, not whispered or mediated. And the people, terrified, cried out for Moses to stand between them and the Voice. They sensed instinctively that this Presence was too weighty, too real, too consuming to encounter casually. Yet God receives their fear with compassion, not frustration: "Oh, that their hearts would be inclined to fear me and keep my commands always."

This passage reveals something profound about God and about us. We're drawn to holiness and frightened by it at the same time. We long for a word that's true, steady, luminous . . . and we also shrink back when that word exposes us. The Israelites feared that hearing God directly would undo them, and in a way, they were right. Encounters with divine truth always undo illusions before they rebuild identity.

So, God meets them in mercy. God doesn't demand that they endure what they can't bear. Instead, God speaks through Moses: drawing near in a way that doesn't overwhelm, guiding them step by step into a life shaped by love and justice. The goal of the law isn't terror but transformation. God desires people who live awake to divine presence, not crushed beneath divine weight.

Spiritually, this passage speaks to our reluctance to let God deeply speak into our lives. So often, I sense a word stirring: an invitation to forgive, to reconcile, to release some idol I've guarded, to pursue a calling I've delayed, and something in me resists. I fear what obedience will cost. I fear what honesty will uncover. But God never speaks to destroy; God speaks to heal, to free, to remake. The voice that once thundered from fire now calls gently through Scripture, prayer, conscience, and community. The invitation is the same: "Walk in all the ways I command you, that it may go well with you."

This passage also reshapes how Christians live in the world. If the God we follow speaks truth that's weighty yet compassionate, then we're called to become a people whose lives echo that balance: truth without cruelty, courage without superiority, humility without silence. We carry a received word, not an invented one; we embody a love that holds both reverence and tenderness. Faithfulness looks like listening deeply before speaking boldly.

And in Jesus, the mystery of this passage reaches its fullness. The people once begged for a mediator, and God answers with one who doesn't merely speak on God's behalf but embodies the very heart of God. In him, the unendurable fire becomes approachable love. The voice that once shook the mountain now whispers courage into fearful hearts.

To follow Jesus is to welcome the divine voice, not as thunder that destroys, but as truth that restores.

Guiding Truth: Let God's voice reshape your heart: listen deeply, walk faithfully, and trust that divine truth always leads toward life.

Reflection: Where am I resisting God's voice because I fear the change it might bring? What steps of obedience is God inviting me to take so that life may "go well" with me and those I love?

Prayer: Holy God, speak again to my hesitant heart. Calm my fear of your truth and draw me into deeper trust. Let your voice heal what I hide, strengthen what I fear, and guide me into the life you desire for me. Keep me close, awake, and willing. Amen.

Day 13: Love That Shapes a Life

Reading: Deuteronomy 6:1–9

Moses turns from law to love, from command to the beating heart beneath every command. Standing before a people on the edge of promise, he speaks the words that would become Israel's daily prayer, the center of faith, the compass for every generation: "Hear, O Israel: the Lord our God, the Lord is one. Love the Lord your God with all your heart and with all your soul and with all your strength."

These verses are revelations. God isn't a distant force or a collection of competing deities. God is One: whole, faithful, undivided. And because God is undivided, our love is meant to be undivided. Heart, soul, strength: the entire person invited into a whole love. Love is the orientation of the entire self toward the One who is worthy.

Moses goes further. These words are to be "on your heart," not pinned to clothing, not filed away in memory, but carried in the quiet interior where identity is formed. They're to be taught to children, spoken at home and on the road, remembered in the morning and before sleep. Faith is meant to saturate ordinary life. The rhythms of daily existence become the liturgy where love is learned.

Spiritually, this passage asks an honest, searching question. It asks: What shapes my heart? What captivates my imagination? Where do I invest my strength? Love for God grows where attention goes. If I give my best energy to anxiety, resentment, achievement, or distraction, that love withers. But when I let divine love ground me (by pausing, breathing, remembering, reciting, and rehearsing the goodness of God), my inner life shifts. My desires begin to heal. My mind steadies. My strength is redeemed.

These verses also redefine what Christian living looks like. Loving God with our whole being spills outward into how we love others. A heart steeped in divine love becomes a heart that seeks peace, speaks truth, practices humility, forgives readily, and embodies compassion. When love for God becomes the center, love for neighbor ceases to be a command we struggle to obey and becomes the natural overflow of a transformed life.

The call to "impress these words on your children" isn't merely about parenting; it's about witness. We pass on the faith not by argument but by embodied love: the way we speak, the way we forgive, the way we pray, the way we live with integrity when no one is watching. The everyday moments (walking, resting, rising) become sacred opportunities to reflect the love we've received.

In Jesus, this command finds its fullest expression. He calls this the greatest commandment because he embodies it perfectly. His life is whole love in motion: heart, soul, strength given without reserve. And through his Spirit, he plants that same love within us, enabling what we can't produce on our own.

To love God entirely is to be healed into wholeness. To follow Jesus is to be drawn into the kind of life where love becomes the air we breathe.

Guiding Truth: Let divine love shape your whole life (heart, soul, body, relationships, service, prayer, and strength) until love becomes your witness in the world.

Reflection: What currently holds the deepest place in my heart, and how might God be inviting me to reorder my loves? How can I weave love for God into the rhythms of my daily life, both inwardly and outwardly?

Prayer: Holy One, gather my scattered loves into one wholehearted devotion. Write your words on my heart, shape my desires, and steady my strength. Let your love take root in me so deeply that it transforms how I live, speak, and serve this day. Amen.

Day 14: Remembering Grace in the Land of Plenty

Reading: Deuteronomy 6:10–25

Moses turns from the command to love God to the coming danger that could erode that love: forgetfulness. The people are about to enter a land bursting with abundance, "great and splendid cities you did not build, houses filled with good things you did not provide, wells you did not dig, vineyards and olive trees you did not plant." These gifts are pure grace. But grace, when forgotten, can become entitlement. Moses warns them: "When you've eaten and are satisfied, be careful that you don't forget the Lord."

This is a striking truth: for many of us, spiritual danger increases not in hardship but in comfort. Hunger teaches us to cry out. Crisis pushes us into prayer. But abundance (ease, security, success) can lull the soul into a state of amnesia. Moses knows this. Forgetfulness leads to drift, drift leads to idolatry, and idolatry leads to bondage all over again. God delivers us from Egypt, but we can recreate Egypt in our hearts if we let gratitude fade.

So, Moses offers a remedy: tell the story. Teach it to your children. When they ask why you live differently, why you worship the unseen God, why you resist the idols others embrace, answer with memory: "We were slaves, but the Lord brought us out with a mighty hand." The cure for pride is remembering that everything (freedom, land, life, hope) is a gift. The cure for idolatry is remembering the God who rescues.

Spiritually, this passage calls us to cultivate a grounded gratitude, a remembering heart. When I forget who delivered me, I begin to trust my own strength, defend my own comfort, and build my own idols. But remembering places me back in truth. I remember that the breath in my lungs is grace, the opportunities before me are grace, the forgiveness that has healed me is grace, and the community that carries me is grace. Gratitude keeps me awake to God; forgetfulness numbs me.

This text also calls us to a life of witness. The next generation won't know the story unless we tell it, and not only with words, but with embodied faithfulness. When our lives blend justice, humility, compassion, and courage, we answer the unspoken question: "What does it mean to belong to God?" When we speak honestly of how God has carried us through our own Egypts, we pass on a faith rooted in real history and real grace.

In Jesus, this passage becomes a living reality. He's the One who frees us from deeper slavery, the One who offers living water we did not dig, the One who prepares a place of abundance we did not earn. In him, the danger of forgetfulness is met with the remedy of remembrance: "Do this in remembrance of me." In his table, his cross, his presence, we learn again to receive everything as a gift.

To live this passage is to let gratitude loosen our grip on wealth, pride, and comfort, and to let love anchor us in the God who gives generously and faithfully.

Guiding Truth: Remember the grace that carried you, gratitude guards the heart and keeps love alive in seasons of abundance.

Reflection: Where has comfort or abundance quietly pulled my heart toward forgetfulness or self-sufficiency? How can I practice remembrance, telling the story of God's grace to myself, my family, or my community?

Prayer: Generous God, keep me from forgetting the love that delivered me. Let gratitude reshape my desires, my habits, and my witness. Teach me to remember your grace in every season and to live as someone formed by mercy, not by pride. Amen.

Day 15: A People Formed by Holy Love

Reading: Deuteronomy 7:1–26

Moses speaks to a people about to enter a land filled with nations stronger than themselves. The command is stark: they're not to absorb the practices, idols, or patterns of those nations. They're to tear down altars, refuse alliances that compromise identity, and guard the covenant with fierce resolve. At first glance, these verses feel harsh, unsettling even. But beneath them lies a burning truth: God is forming a people shaped by holy love, and such formation can't coexist with the idols that deform hearts.

The call to separation isn't about superiority. Moses says plainly: "The Lord didn't set affection on you because you were numerous . . . but because the Lord loved you." The foundation of Israel's identity is God's abundant and surprising grace. They're chosen not for greatness but for love; treasured not for merit but for mercy. Their holiness is God's gracious gift, and a response to divine character and love.

The danger Moses warns against is spiritual assimilation. The idols of Canaan weren't harmless artifacts; they represented entire systems of injustice, violence, exploitation, and fear. To embrace those gods would be to adopt those practices. God is protecting human dignity. Holiness is the shield that keeps a community from becoming what it was liber-ated from.

Spiritually, this passage presses gently but firmly on our own compromises. God asks us to name the idols that seduce us: not carved images, but any desire or attachment that reorders our loves away from the One who frees. The idol of success that reshapes identity. The idol of security that closes the fist. The idol of approval that silences truth. The idol of pleasure that numbs the soul. These idols rarely arrive with a roar; they creep in through affection, habit, or convenience. Moses' call ("Don't give your heart to them") reminds us that what we love, we eventually resemble.

Moses then goes on to bless. He speaks of a God who keeps covenant, who pours out steadfast love to a thousand generations of those who walk in fidelity. Holiness, then, is joyful belonging. It's the life that flows from knowing we're held, chosen, cherished. When divine love takes root, obedience becomes desire, not duty.

This passage also shapes how Christians live. We're called not to withdraw from the world but to resist its dehumanizing ways. To practice compassion when others practice consumption. To choose humility where pride is celebrated. To forgive instead of retaliating, to serve rather than dominate, to love even where the world offers contempt. Holiness is presence transformed by love. It's living in a way that allows others to glimpse the freedom, shalom, and justice of God's kingdom.

In Jesus, the beauty of this chapter shines brighter. He's the Holy One who enters a world of idols and refuses every temptation. He loves without compromise and saves without violence. He forms a people whose holiness reflects the heart of God: courageous, compassionate, self-giving. His cross breaks the power of every idol; his love calls us into a life where holiness is freedom.

Guiding Truth: Let divine love shape you so fully that every idol loses its grip and your life reflects the freedom of holiness.

Reflection: What subtle idols (habits, desires, or fears) compete for my deepest love and loyalty? How can I practice a holiness that looks like Jesus: compassionate, courageous, self-giving, and free?

Prayer: Holy One, reveal the idols that dull my love and divide my heart. Tear down what enslaves me and restore me to the freedom of belonging to you. Let your love reshape my desires and my life, so I may walk in holiness that heals and blesses the world. Amen.

Day 16: The Wilderness That Teaches Us to Live

Reading: Deuteronomy 8:1–20

Moses speaks tenderly yet urgently to a people on the threshold of abundance. Before them lies a land of streams, vineyards, wheat, honey, and flourishing. Behind them lies a wilderness of hunger, thirst, and wandering. But Moses insists the wilderness was not wasted. It was the place where God humbled them, tested them, fed them, sustained them, and taught them that life doesn't emerge from bread alone but from every word that comes from the mouth of the Holy One.

This chapter is a spiritual anatomy of memory. Moses wants the people to know that the wilderness was their teacher. In scarcity, they learned to depend on each other. In the hunger, they discovered manna: food they had never known, food that reminded them daily that they lived by gift, not by achievement. In their fragility, they discovered a God who carried them as one carries a beloved child. The wilderness stripped away false securities so that trust could grow deep roots.

But the danger ahead is subtle and far more seductive: abundance. Prosperity carries within it a quiet spiritual erosion. Moses warns them that when they eat and are satisfied, when their houses are full, and their fields yield fruit, they may forget the One who brought them out of bondage. Forgetfulness is a slow untethering. It begins when gratitude fades, and pride grows, when the heart says, "My strength has produced this."

Spiritually, this passage asks us to reckon with our own wildernesses and our own comforts. Many of us (perhaps unknowingly) were shaped most deeply in the seasons we wanted least. Wildernesses taught us to pray honestly, cling desperately, and listen attentively. They revealed our limits and God's constancy. But comfort can dull us. Abundance can make prayer optional. Fullness can make trust seem unnecessary. Moses' warning is a mercy: don't forget the God who held you when nothing else could.

This chapter also teaches us how to live as people formed by grace. Gratitude becomes a safeguard. Remembrance becomes resistance. Humility becomes worship. To remember that "it's God who gives you the ability to produce" anything (wisdom, strength, resources, influence) is to live with open hands rather than clenched fists. Such remembrance produces generosity, justice, compassion, and humility. It frees us from the tyranny of self-made identity and anchors us in a love that precedes and sustains us.

And in Jesus, we see the deepest truth of this chapter. In his own wilderness, he answers the tempter with words drawn from Deuteronomy 8: "We don't live by bread alone." He shows us that true life flows not from possession or security but from communion with God. His life embodies the humility Israel was called to: the refusal to grasp power, the embrace of dependence, the daily trust in the Father's faithfulness. He leads us into a freedom where abundance becomes generosity, and memory becomes worship.

The invitation of Deuteronomy 8 is simple and searching: remember. Remember the God who sustained you in scarcity. Remember the grace that brought you through. Remember that everything is a gift. And let that remembrance shape your life into a testimony of gratitude and trust.

Guiding Truth: Remember who carried you in the wilderness, so abundance never becomes forgetfulness.

Reflection: What wilderness experiences has God used to deepen my trust and reshape my heart? In what ways might abundance, comfort, or success be tempting me toward spiritual forgetfulness?

Prayer: Faithful God, teach me to remember. In abundance, keep me grateful; in scarcity, keep me trusting. Guard my heart from pride and forgetfulness, and let every season draw me deeper into love, humility, and dependence on you. Amen.

Day 17: The God Who Saves Us From Ourselves

Reading: Deuteronomy 9:1–29

Moses speaks with a sobering clarity. Israel is about to cross the Jordan and face nations stronger, larger, and more fortified than anything they've known. Yet the real danger is the pride that waits within their own hearts. Moses understands the human impulse to rewrite the story, to imagine that victory comes from personal virtue, that blessing is earned, that chosenness is a reward. So he says: "Not because of your righteousness . . . but because of the Lord's promise."

This chapter is one of the most humbling in Scripture. Moses forces Israel to remember their history truthfully: the golden calf, the rebellion at Kadesh, the grumbling, the stubbornness. He recounts moments when God nearly wiped them out, and how he lay prostrate before God (forty days and nights) pleading for mercy. Israel stands before promise only because God is faithful, patient, and committed to a covenant they couldn't keep on their own.

These verses strip away illusion. We stand in grace because God keeps remembering us even when we forget God. Moses wants the people to walk into the land with humility, not swagger, with gratitude, not entitlement, and with reverence, not self-congratulation. A proud heart can't hold the weight of divine promise; it cracks under the illusion of self-made righteousness.

Spiritually, this passage invites a kind of honest self-reckoning. Moses' recounting of Israel's failures is designed to awaken hearts. Memory becomes the soil of humility. When I remember the places where my heart wandered, where fear made me small, where ego distorted my choices, I remember also the mercy that carried me anyway. Confession clears space for gratitude. Humility becomes the doorway through which grace flows freely.

Moses' intercession is central to this chapter. While the people were shaping idols, he lay face down, pleading with them. He prayed until mercy prevailed. This is what love looks like in a broken community, standing in the gap, refusing to let failure have the last word, holding others before God with compassion rather than condemnation. It's a picture of what Christian life requires: patience with the stumbling, prayer for the stubborn, forgiveness for those who wound us, a refusal to give up on people because God has not given up on us.

And in Jesus, this truth becomes radiant. Moses stood between an angry people and a holy God, but Jesus stands between a broken humanity and a God whose holiness is love. He becomes the intercessor whose prayers never cease. He bears our failures without resentment. He carries our stubbornness without withdrawing his compassion. Where Israel provoked divine anger, Jesus absorbs it. Where Moses wrestled for mercy, Jesus embodies it.

This chapter calls us to walk with humility, to trust grace more than performance, to remember our story truthfully, and to extend to others the same mercy that has held us.

Guiding Truth: Remember who you were and who saved you, so pride never replaces gratitude, and mercy becomes your way of life.

Reflection: Where am I tempted to take credit for what's purely grace in my life? Who is God calling me to hold in compassion and prayer, just as Moses interceded for Israel?

Prayer: Merciful God, save me from the pride that forgets my own story. Teach me to live with humility, gratitude, and compassion. Let your grace define my past, steady my present, and guide my steps so that I may become a person shaped by mercy, not by merit. Amen.

Day 18: When God Writes on Our Hearts Again

Reading: Deuteronomy 10:1–11

After the crushing failure of the golden calf, Moses retells one of the most astonishing moments in Israel's story. God calls him back up the mountain, not to condemn the people again, but to begin again. "Chisel out two stone tablets like the first," God says, "and I'll write on them what was on the first tablets that you broke."

These words are a miracle of mercy. God doesn't abandon the covenant. God rewrites it. The tablets Moses shattered in righteous anger become a symbol not of divine rejection but of divine determination. Even after betrayal, God initiates restoration. The covenant is a vow held by a God who refuses to let failure have the final say.

Moses builds an ark to hold the new tablets. The symbol is deliberate and tender. Israel's restored relationship is something to be carried, guarded, and treasured. God is forming a people who understand grace not as a vague sentiment but as something inscribed: concrete, lasting, carried in the center of the camp.

This passage tells us something essential about spiritual life: God meets us in the places we've broken trust. Our failures don't push God away; they draw God into deeper restoring work. Where we see rubble and regret, God sees a new beginning. The God who writes again on stone writes again on the heart. Every moment of repentance becomes an opening for divine compassion to carve something new into us.

Moses also reminds the people of God's continuous care: the priestly ministry of the Levites, the inheritance given to them, and the travels through the wilderness where God remained near. Restoration is a sustained posture of grace. God forgives, calls, provides, and leads, over and over.

Spiritually, this passage invites us to let God rewrite what we've broken. There are places in each of us (relationships, habits, choices, and patterns) where the tablets have shattered. Shame may suggest that we've gone too far, that we've ruined what can't be repaired. But this text proclaims a different truth: God restores covenant even in the wake of betrayal. Forgiveness is the doorway back into life. Renewal is God's delight.

Such wisdom also shapes how Christians live in the world. If God rewrites covenant after our worst failures, then we're invited to become people of renewal rather than condemnation, people who believe in second chances, and people who hold space for others to repent, rebuild, and return. God invites us to be people who refuse to define others by their lowest moment. To follow Jesus is to embody mercy that rewrites stories rather than repeating accusations.

And Jesus himself is the fullest expression of this mountain moment. He doesn't just rewrite a broken covenant; he becomes the covenant. In him, the divine word takes flesh. In him, the law is fulfilled, transformed, and written on hearts by the Spirit. Through him, God says to all of us who have shattered what was given: "Come up the mountain again. We begin anew."

Guiding Truth: Let God rewrite what's been broken: grace always rises where repentance opens the heart.

Reflection: What "shattered tablets" in my life is God inviting me to bring back up the mountain for restoration? How can I embody God's renewing mercy toward someone who needs a fresh beginning?

Prayer: God of new beginnings, write on my heart again. Heal what I've broken, restore what's been lost, and shape me by your mercy. Teach me to receive your grace without fear and to extend that same grace to others. Make my life a testimony of renewal. Amen.

Day 19: The Heart of Covenant Life

Reading: Deuteronomy 10:12–22

Moses gathers the whole wilderness story into a few breathtaking lines: "What does the Lord your God ask of you?" It's a question that pierces through ritual, fear, tradition, and complexity. And the answer is disarmingly simple and impossibly profound: fear God, walk in God's ways, love God, serve God with your whole being, and keep the commands given for your flourishing.

These words are a portrait of a life shaped by holy love. Moses begins with awe, "fear God," not a cowering dread but a reverent awareness that steadies the soul. Awe anchors obedience. Then comes walking in God's ways: aligning ordinary life with divine character. Loving God with heart and soul. Serving God with the whole self. Obeying not as a burden, but as a path toward life.

Moses grounds all of this in identity, not obligation. God owns the heavens and the earth, yet shows affection for Israel. Not because they were numerous, powerful, or impressive, but because divine love chooses freely. The commands of God begin with the heart of God, and the heart of God is delight.

Then Moses turns the command inward: "Circumcise your hearts." This is one of the earliest biblical calls to inner transformation. God wants hearts that are tender, unclenched, unarmored. Hearts that aren't shaped by stubbornness, resentment, or pride. Hearts capable of receiving love and giving love. Holiness begins not with external performance but with an interior reshaping, a surrender of self-protective barriers so that grace can carve something new.

And what does a circumcised heart look like in the world? Moses answers with clarity: care for the stranger, defend the vulnerable, love those who don't yet belong. The God who rescued Israel when they were helpless commands them to embody the same compassion. Divine love isn't tribal; it's expansive, boundary-shattering. God "loves the stranger" and therefore calls God's people to do the same. Holiness is hospitality.

Spiritually, this passage forces us to ask whether our devotion flows outward. If our love for God remains private or theoretical, it hasn't yet reached the heart. A heart shaped by divine tenderness becomes generous, just, courageous, and compassionate. It sees the ignored, welcomes the outsider, and stands with the vulnerable. The more we remember the grace that found us, the more freely we give that grace away.

And in Jesus, this call becomes incarnate. He embodies every word Moses speaks: awe-filled trust in the Father, walking in divine ways, love beyond measure, service without reserve. His heart (wide open, pierced for the world) becomes the model and the means of our own transformation. Through him, hearts of stone become hearts of flesh. Through him, the love of God is written into us, not just commanded of us.

This passage insists that true covenant life is always love in motion: vertical awe shaping horizontal compassion, devotion shaping justice, worship shaping welcome.

Guiding Truth: Let God reshape your heart so profoundly that love for God flows naturally into love for the stranger.

Reflection: Where is my heart still guarded, resistant, or closed, and how might God be inviting me to open it? Who is the "stranger" or overlooked person God is calling me to love with concrete compassion?

Prayer: Tender God, soften my heart. Strip away what resists your love and reshape me into someone who reflects your compassion. Teach me to walk in your ways, love as you love, and welcome those you welcome. Make my life a witness to your justice and mercy. Amen.

Day 20: Loving God With Your Whole Life

Reading: Deuteronomy 11:1–21

Moses stands before a people who have seen much (discipline, deliverance, rebellion, manna, fire, mercy), and he invites them into the heart of covenant life: "Love the Lord your God and keep God's requirements . . . so that you may be strong." Strength, in this vision, is persevering love: the kind that stays faithful through seasons of scarcity and seasons of abundance.

Moses reminds them of what their own eyes have witnessed: the signs in Egypt, the parting of the sea, the guidance in the wilderness, the discipline that shaped them into a people who can bear blessing. He tells them that love is lived memory. Obedience is the shape love takes when we remember who carried us.

Then Moses casts a striking contrast between Egypt and the promised land. Egypt was a place where life depended on human labor: watering the fields with foot-pumped irrigation, enduring oppressive systems, and surviving through relentless effort. But the new land is different. It drinks rain from heaven. God's own care tends it. Flourishing in this land requires trust, not toil; communion, not control. It's a place where dependence on God is a gift.

Spiritually, this passage invites us to examine where "Egypt" still clings to our hearts. Egypt is any way of living that depends solely on our own strength, where anxiety becomes our engine, performance becomes our identity, and self-reliance becomes our refuge. The promised land is trust: daily dependence that frees us from the illusions of self-sufficiency.

Moses then speaks of the inner work required: "Fix these words of mine in your heart and mind." Love for God is cultivated through attention. What we meditate on shapes us. What we remember forms us. Moses urges the people to bind these words on their hands and foreheads, teach them to their children, speak them at home and on the road, because the daily drip of remembrance sustains faith.

This passage also shapes how we live with others. Loving God with heart and soul spills into love for neighbor. It softens the harsh, steadies the anxious, enlarges compassion, and anchors humility. When the commands are on our hearts, we become people who live truthfully and generously. Our homes become places where grace is practiced. Our communities become spaces where justice takes root.

In the crescendo of the passage, Moses promises blessing as the fruit of aligning life with God's ways. He describes a land flowing with abundance, a life saturated with divine presence. And for Christians, this promise draws us toward Jesus, the One who embodies the life God desires for us. He frees us from the Egypt of sin and self, invites us into a new way of being, and writes God's law not on tablets but on hearts. In him, we discover that obedience is joyful belonging.

Guiding Truth: Fix God's words on your heart, letting love, trust, and remembrance reshape the way you live each day.

Reflection: Where am I still living with an "Egypt mindset," trusting my own strength instead of resting in God's care? What practices can help me keep God's words before me so that love shapes my daily life?

Prayer: Faithful God, anchor my heart in your love. Free me from self-reliance and teach me to trust your care. Fix your words within me so my life reflects your compassion, justice, and grace. Make my days a witness to the goodness of belonging to you. Strengthen my will when I grow weary, and steady my spirit when fear rises within me. Let your presence shape my choices, my relationships, and my inner life. Form in me a love that endures, a trust that deepens, and a heart that reflects your kindness in all things. Amen.

Day 21: Choosing the Way That Leads to Life

Reading: Deuteronomy 11:22–32

Moses speaks with the clarity of someone who knows how fragile the human heart can be. The people stand on the brink of a new land, a new identity, a new future. But before they cross the Jordan, Moses places two paths before them, the blessing and the curse, life and loss, flourishing and fragmentation. These are invitations. The shape of Israel's future will depend on the posture of Israel's heart.

Moses roots this choice in relationship: "If you carefully keep all these commands, love the Lord your God, walk in all God's ways, and hold fast . . . " These words reveal a pattern of faithfulness. Love comes first. Obedience flows from love. Walking in God's ways flows from obedience. Holding fast flows from trust. Covenant life is about wholehearted attachment to the God who has never let them go.

He describes a stunning promise: if they cling to God's ways, no force can stand against them, because God's presence will steady them. Their strength comes from belonging. Even the smallest community becomes unshakeable when it's rooted in divine faithfulness.

Then Moses gives a tactile sign: the blessing on Mount Gerizim, the curse on Mount Ebal. These mountains will stand as witnesses, visible reminders that their choices matter. The Holy One honors their freedom and places before them a real decision: Will you walk the path of love, trust, and obedience, or drift into the way of forgetfulness and self-reliance?

Every day, multiple times, we stand at our own Gerizim and Ebal. Will I move toward forgiveness or toward resentment? Toward truth or toward compromise? Toward compassion or toward numbness? Toward trust or toward self-protection? The blessing is the natural fruit of a life aligned with divine love. The curse is the collapse that happens when we build on foundations too small to hold us.

This text calls us to attentiveness. To recognize that our habits shape our hearts, our hearts shape our choices, and our choices shape our lives. Faith is a thousand small decisions that bend us toward love or away from it. Moses' words awaken us, reminding us that life with God is a living relationship that flourishes when we hold fast.

And in Jesus, this invitation becomes clearer still. He speaks of two paths, two foundations, two ways of seeing the world. He calls us again and again to choose life, choose love, choose the narrow way that leads to freedom. He embodies the blessing, showing what it looks like when a human life is wholly aligned with God's will. And through him, we receive the grace that empowers our obedience, the mercy that restores us when we choose poorly, and the Spirit that strengthens us to walk in love.

Guiding Truth: Choose the path of love and trust each day: every small decision can bend your life toward blessing.

Reflection: What choices, large or small, am I facing right now that call me to choose between trust and self-reliance? How can I "hold fast" to God today in a practical, embodied way?

Prayer: Holy God, teach me to choose the way that leads to life. Keep my heart awake to your presence, my mind aligned with your truth, and my steps steady in your love. Guard me from the drift of forgetfulness, and strengthen me to walk the path of blessing with courage and humility. Amen.

Day 22: Worship That Shapes a Way of Life

Reading: Deuteronomy 12:1–32

As Israel prepares to enter the land, Moses turns their attention to the beating heart of their identity: worship. Before they build cities, before they plant fields, before they settle into the rhythms of ordinary life, they must decide how and whom they'll worship. Everything else flows from that choice.

God commands them to tear down the altars, pillars, shrines, and idols of the nations they'll encounter. Not because God fears competition, but because these forms of worship are rooted in practices that dehumanize, exploit, and distort. False gods always demand life from their worshipers. The true God gives life. Moses insists that the place of worship must be chosen by God, not invented by the people. Worship is communion and a response.

This chapter reveals something profound: worship shapes the whole of life. Israel's sacrifices, festivals, offerings, and gatherings are rhythms that form them into a people who know how to receive and give love. In a world of violent altars and anxious sacrifice, Israel is invited into joy: eating, rejoicing, feasting before God. Holiness is about learning to enjoy God's gifts without turning them into idols.

Moses tells them not to worship "in every place that you see." This is a warning against do-it-yourself spirituality, the temptation to create a faith that costs nothing, challenges nothing, and asks nothing.

True worship reorients the heart. It breaks our allegiance to lesser loves. It turns us toward justice, humility, gratitude, and compassion. It anchors us in the God whose love frees us from fear.

Spiritually, this passage confronts us with our own altars. What are the places where my heart wanders? What do I turn to for security, identity, or control? What habits distort my loves? God's call isn't to tear down beauty but to tear down bondage. The altars God asks us to dismantle are the ones that deform the soul: addictions, resentments, compulsions, obsessions, false desires. Removing them creates room for devotion that heals rather than harms.

Moses also urges the people to rejoice in God's presence. This is essential. Obedience is feast-like. It's celebrating the One who provides, sustains, forgives, and restores. Worship becomes the wellspring from which justice flows: when our hearts are rightly oriented toward God, our lives become shaped by compassion, generosity, truthfulness, and peace.

And here, too, we see Christ. He becomes the place where God chooses to dwell. No longer tied to a single location, worship centers on a person: one whose life reveals the heart of God and whose Spirit leads us into true devotion. He teaches us that worship is transformation. It's becoming like the One we adore.

Deuteronomy 12 invites us into a life where worship is the continual turning of the heart toward the God who frees us, forms us, and fills our lives with joy.

Guiding Truth: Tear down the altars that diminish you, and let true worship reshape your heart toward joy, justice, and love.

Reflection: What "altars" or attachments might God be calling me to dismantle so I can love more freely and live more fully? How can I let worship (daily gratitude, prayer, joy, and obedience) reshape my life this week?

Prayer: Holy One, turn my heart fully toward you. Dismantle every false love that binds me, and form me through worship that's joyful, humble, and true. Teach me to love what you love and to live in ways shaped by your presence and compassion. Amen.

Day 23: Guarding the Heart With Courage and Love

Reading: Deuteronomy 13:1–18

This chapter is one of the most sobering in Deuteronomy. Moses speaks to a people about to enter a land filled with spiritual allure, prophets who perform signs yet speak false words, trusted friends who whisper seductive invitations, and communities tempted to drift into worship that destroys rather than heals. The concern here is devotion. God is shaping a people whose hearts are wholly turned toward the One who brought them out of slavery.

Moses warns of three threats: the charismatic deceiver, the intimate persuader, and the collective drift of a town that abandons the covenant. In every case, the danger is subtle. The false prophet may look impressive. The loved one may feel trustworthy. The town may still appear peaceful. But anything that leads Israel toward gods of violence, exploitation, and fear threatens to unravel everything God has formed in them.

The language is fierce because the stakes are high. Idolatry in the ancient world was embracing systems that normalized oppression, sexual violence, child sacrifice, and the dehumanization of the vulnerable. To follow those gods was to unlearn justice and forget compassion. Moses calls Israel to resist these pullings with clarity, courage, and unwavering fidelity. Not out of hatred for others, but out of love for the God who rescues, and love for the community whose life depends on truth.

Spiritually, this chapter asks us to be honest about the voices that influence us. False prophets still exist, though they rarely claim the title. They surface as ideologies that promise life but erode character; as leaders who charm but don't love; as habits that numb the soul while presenting themselves as freedom. Moses' call is to discernment: to measure every voice against the truth, beauty, and goodness of God's character.

The challenge grows sharper when Moses speaks of persuasion coming from the people closest to us. Here, he names the tender reality that loyalty can be misplaced. We sometimes follow people we love into patterns that quietly deform us. The call is to courage, to love others without surrendering the truth that anchors us, to remain faithful even when affection pulls us in another direction.

This chapter also speaks to the communal responsibility of faith. When a whole town drifts from God's ways, the community must confront the drift. Not through cruelty or self-righteousness, but through the hard work of naming falsehood, restoring truth, and protecting the vulnerable. Faith is communal. The flourishing of one affects the flourishing of all.

And in Jesus, this passage finds its deepest fulfillment. He confronts falsehood with wisdom. He resists temptation with truth. He exposes destructive patterns and invites repentance, restoration, and new life. He teaches a holiness that's compassionate, courageous, and discerning. He guards our hearts by anchoring us in love that can't be shaken.

To live this passage is to cultivate a heart both tender and wise, a heart that refuses to follow voices that lead toward fear, injustice, or idolatry, and instead cleaves to the One whose voice brings life.

Guiding Truth: Guard your heart with love and discernment: cling to the God who frees, and refuse every voice that leads away from life.

Reflection: What voices (cultural, relational, internal) may be subtly pulling my heart away from the truth and compassion of God? How can I cultivate a discerning love that stays faithful to God while loving others deeply and well?

Prayer: Holy God, steady my heart in your truth. Guard me from false voices and lead me into wisdom that's humble, courageous, and full of love. Form in me a devotion that clings to you and a compassion that reflects your heart to others. Amen.

Day 24: Becoming What We Feast On

Reading: Deuteronomy 14:1–21

Moses begins this section with a stunning reminder of identity: "You're children of the Lord your God." Before he gives a single instruction about food, he grounds everything in belonging. Israel is defined by relationship. The call to holiness begins with remembering who they are and whose they are.

From that identity flows the call to distinctiveness. Israel is instructed not to imitate the mourning practices of surrounding nations and not to consume foods associated with impurity. These commands can seem obscure or distant to us, but their purpose is profoundly relational and formational. God is teaching Israel to live as a people set apart: not set above others, but set apart for a different way of being in the world.

The nations around them practiced rituals shaped by fear, superstition, manipulation, and attempts to control the unseen. God wants none of that for Israel. Their identity is grounded in righteousness, holiness, and trust. Their lives are to reflect the character of the One who calls them beloved. Thus, the laws about food serve as daily reminders that holiness is found in ordinary life. Every meal becomes a small act of devotion, a training in discernment, and a practice in remembering the One who provides.

Spiritually, this passage reminds us that formation happens through repetition. What we consume (physically, emotionally, spiritually) every ordinary day shapes us. The question beneath this text is piercing: What am I feeding my soul? And what's it making me become?

We become like what we consume. If we feed on resentment, we become bitter. If we feed on fear, we become anxious. If we feed on comparison, we become restless. But if we feed on God's presence, on truth, on gratitude, on love, then holiness becomes not an achievement but a natural growth.

Moses reminds the people again: "You're a people holy to the Lord your God." Holiness here is belonging and identity rooted in grace. These dietary practices are about remembering that all of life (eating, grieving, celebrating) is meant to reflect the God who claimed them in love.

And in Jesus, the heart of this chapter finds its most profound meaning. He teaches that it isn't what enters the mouth that defiles a person, but what emerges from the heart. He shifts the emphasis from external purity to internal transformation. Yet he also calls us to practices that form us, habits of fasting, feasting, prayer, gratitude, and mercy that shape who we become. His table becomes the place of our re-formation, where bread and cup train our hearts to desire what's true and good.

This passage invites us to discern our daily habits of consumption (literal and metaphorical) so that our lives reflect the holiness of the One who loves us. In a world full of spiritual diets that malnourish the soul, God calls us to feast on what leads to life.

Guiding Truth: Feed your life with what reflects God's love; what you consume will shape who you become.

Reflection: What habits, influences, or desires am I "feeding on" that shape my heart in ways that don't reflect God's love? What daily practices could nourish holiness, gratitude, and compassion in me this week?

Prayer: Holy One, teach me to hunger for what leads to life. Turn my heart from whatever diminishes your image in me, and nourish me with truth, love, and wisdom. Shape my daily habits so that I become someone who reflects your compassion and holiness in all things. Amen.

Day 25: Generosity That Opens the Heart

Reading: Deuteronomy 14:22–29

Moses turns from matters of holiness and identity to the practical rhythms that sustain a just and compassionate community. The practice at the center of this passage is tithing, setting aside a portion of one's harvest each year. This is a spiritual formation practice, a reorientation of the heart around abundance, gratitude, and shared life.

Israel is called to bring a tenth of their produce to "the place God will choose," not simply to give it away, but to eat it before the Lord with joy. This is extraordinary. The tithe isn't only an offering; it's a feast. Worship is imagined as a communal celebration. God is teaching Israel to see provision as a gift, not a possession, to delight in grace rather than hoard resources in fear.

But the command goes deeper. If the journey to the sanctuary is too long, they may convert their harvest into silver and purchase food and drink at the refuge itself, so long as they rejoice in God's presence. The emphasis is on the heart: gratitude expressed as joy, generosity expressed as worship.

Then Moses shifts the focus outward: every third year, the tithe is stored locally so that the Levites, the strangers, the orphans, and the widows may eat and be satisfied. Here, generosity becomes justice. God builds into Israel's agricultural rhythm a system of care for the most vulnerable. No one is to be forgotten. No one is to be left hungry.

Abundance is never meant to terminate on the one who receives it. It must flow outward, like the heart of God.

Spiritually, this passage invites us to examine how we hold what we have. Do I see my resources (money, time, gifts, opportunities) as mine to protect or ours to share? Gratitude expands the heart; fear shrinks it. The tithe is about cultivating a posture of open-handedness before God and neighbor. It trains us to trust that provision will continue, that generosity won't bankrupt us, that abundance is multiplied when shared.

This text also reminds us that worship and justice are inseparable. To feast before God while ignoring the hungry at our gate is unthinkable in the biblical vision. True worship opens the heart toward the vulnerable. True generosity restores dignity. Genuine gratitude bends outward.

We see this lived perfectly in Jesus. He welcomes people experiencing poverty to his table, multiplies bread for those experiencing hunger, and teaches that where our treasure is, our hearts will follow. He models a generosity that's joyful, abundant, and rooted in trust. His life reveals that giving isn't loss but participation in the overflowing life of God.

Deuteronomy 14 calls us into a way of being where generosity is a rhythm of life, where joy and justice mingle, where our resources become instruments of love, and where our hearts are shaped into reflections of God's own generosity.

Guiding Truth: Give with joy and open hands: generosity forms the heart and makes God's abundance visible in the world.

Reflection: Where might fear or scarcity-thinking be constricting my generosity: financially, emotionally, or relationally? How can I cultivate practices of joyful giving that reflect God's heart for the vulnerable?

Prayer: Generous God, teach me to hold all I have with open hands. Free me from fear, deepen my gratitude, and let my giving become an act of joy and justice. Shape my heart so that your abundance flows through me to those in need. Amen.

Day 26: Freedom, Generosity, and the Heart Set Loose

Reading: Deuteronomy 15:1–18

Every seven years, God commands a rhythm that disrupts every empire-shaped instinct within us: debts are forgiven, enslaved people are released, and abundance is shared without hesitation. This is covenant made manifest. God knows the human heart, knows how easily greed takes root, knows how quickly systems become unjust. So God builds into Israel's life a cycle of liberation that reflects the divine heartbeat: freedom, mercy, restoration.

Moses speaks plainly: "There shouldn't be people experiencing poverty among you." Not because poverty will never appear, but because the community's response to need is meant to be so immediate, so generous, so joyful, that poverty is never allowed to harden into permanence. The land belongs to God. The harvest is a gift. Wealth is stewardship, not entitlement. In a world that normalizes scarcity and hoarding, God calls Israel to practice a culture of release.

Debt is forgiven: not postponed, not renegotiated, but erased. The one who has fallen behind is restored to dignity. This is a radical recalibration of worth. In God's economy, a person is never reduced to what they owe. The sabbatical year insists that the story of someone in need isn't defined by lack but by belonging.

Enslaved people (typically fellow Israelites who entered servitude because of debt) are freed after six years, and not sent away empty-handed. God commands the community to furnish them generously from their own flocks, grain, and wine. Liberation is a feast of restoration. God reminds them: "Remember that you were slaves in Egypt and the Lord redeemed you." Their generosity must rise from the memory that humility and compassion grow from knowing you've been rescued, too.

Spiritually, this passage confronts the tight places in our hearts. It presses on the instinct to cling, to protect, to calculate. God calls us to a generosity shaped by hope, love, and freedom. The deeper invitation is this: let your heart be trained by mercy, not scarcity. Release resentment. Release control. Release the need to get even. Release whatever chains another person. Freedom flows in both directions, toward the one set loose and toward the one who loosens the grip.

And this passage points us toward a prophetic life of justice. Caring for people experiencing poverty is a covenant. God anchors compassion in identity. A community that practices release embodies the heart of God to a watching world, where forgiveness is normal, where generosity is joyful, and where restoration is expected.

In Jesus, we witness the fullness of this rhythm. He proclaims release to the captives, cancels spiritual debts, lifts shame from the shoulders of the broken, and reshapes communities into places of grace. His cross becomes the great sabbatical act, where debts we could never repay are forgiven, and where we receive fullness upon fullness. He sends his followers into the world as people who practice this same release, reshaping economies of fear into economies of love.

Guiding Truth: Let mercy train your heart, release freely, give generously, and let God's freedom flow through you.

Reflection: What debts (emotional, relational, or practical) am I still holding onto that God may be inviting me to release? Where can my generosity move from cautious calculation toward joyful, memory-shaped compassion?

Prayer: God of freedom, loosen my heart from fear and scarcity. Teach me to release as I've been released, to give as I've been given, and to restore others with the same mercy you've poured over me. Make my life a witness to your liberating love. Amen.

Day 27: Remembering the Story That Makes Us Free

Reading: Deuteronomy 16:1–17

Moses turns to the great festivals, the sacred rhythms that'll shape Israel's memory, identity, and communal life. Passover, the Festival of Weeks, and the Festival of Booths are acts of remembering, practices of joy, and public rehearsals of the story that formed them. God knows that a forgetful people becomes a fearful people. So God gives them celebrations that anchor them in truth and keep their hearts awake.

Passover calls them to remember deliverance, the night God broke Egypt's grip and led them toward freedom. They eat bread without yeast to remember haste, and they sacrifice the Passover lamb to remember mercy. Every year, they relive the night they were rescued, the night darkness turned to dawn. This memory forms humility and gratitude: "You were once slaves, and God brought you out."

The Festival of Weeks, Pentecost, invites them to bring the first fruits of their harvest. Not leftovers, not what's convenient, but the best. They come with joy, with open hands, with gratitude that all abundance flows from God's generosity. And they're commanded to rejoice, not alone but with neighbors, workers, the poor, the widow, the orphan, the foreigner. This feast unites the entire community. Abundance is meant to be shared. Joy is meant to be collective.

Then comes the Festival of Booths, a weeklong remembrance of wilderness life, when Israel lived in fragile shelters and survived on God's daily provision. By living in temporary huts each year, they remember that security never comes from walls, savings, or possessions; it comes from the One who walked with them through hunger, danger, and thirst. This festival trains them in gratitude, humility, and dependence.

Spiritually, this passage reminds us that we become what we remember. If we remember only scarcity, we become anxious. If we remember our achievements, we become proud. If we remember our wounds, we become hardened. But if we remember God's deliverance, provision, and care, our hearts soften, our lives open, and joy becomes possible again.

God commands Israel to celebrate with joy because joy itself is an act of resistance. It resists despair, greed, individualism, and fear. To feast before God is to proclaim that goodness still holds the world, that mercy still rises, that love is stronger than loss. These festivals declare that suffering doesn't get the last word.

And each of these festivals finds its fullness in Jesus. He's the Passover Lamb whose sacrifice liberates us. He's the first fruits of resurrection, the giver of the Spirit poured out at Pentecost. He's the One who journeys with us through every wilderness, dwelling in our fragile tents of flesh and leading us toward the new creation. When we remember him, we remember the story that makes us free.

This passage invites us to cultivate rhythms that train our hearts, practices of gratitude, generosity, sharing, joy, and remembrance. Holiness is sustained by grace, community, willpower, and patterns that root us in the God who delivers, sustains, and blesses.

Guiding Truth: Remember God's deliverance with joy, let gratitude and shared celebration reshape your heart and your community.

Reflection: What memories am I allowing to shape my life, fearful ones or redemptive ones? What rhythms of gratitude, celebration, or sharing might God be inviting me to practice more intentionally?

Prayer: God of deliverance, teach me to remember your goodness with joy. Root my life in gratitude, steady me in dependence, and open my hands in generosity. Let my rhythms reflect your faithfulness and my celebrations bear witness to your love. Amen.

Day 28: A Community Shaped by Justice, Truth, and Humble Authority

Reading: Deuteronomy 16:18–17:20

As Israel prepares to enter the land, God turns their attention not only to worship but to the kind of society they'll build. Moses speaks of judges, priests, kings, and communal discernment, roles that carry power, influence, and the capacity to either heal or harm. At the center of all these instructions is a single truth: a community that belongs to God must reflect God's justice, God's truth, and God's humility.

Moses begins with judges: "Appoint judges . . . and they must judge the people fairly." No bribes. No favoritism. No bending the truth for personal advantage. In God's kingdom, justice doesn't lean toward the powerful; it leans toward truth. Moses names injustice for what it is: corrosive to the soul and destructive to the community. Justice is covenantal; it's the way people bear witness to the God who rescued them.

Then Moses warns against corrupt worship: altars to false gods, carved images, practices that distort desire and degrade dignity. A community's spiritual life and its ethics can't be separated. If the heart bows to idols, the hands will eventually commit injustice. Idolatry and oppression always walk together.

Next, Moses turns to discernment under challenging cases. When matters exceed human wisdom, they're brought to the priests and judges. The point is humility: no one leads alone. A just society depends on shared discernment, reverence before God's law, and willingness to submit to wisdom outside oneself.

Finally, Moses speaks of the king Israel may one day ask for. The king mustn't accumulate horses (military strength), wives (political alliances), or wealth (economic dominance). Instead, the king must write out a copy of the law, keep it close, read it daily, and let it humble the heart. In other words, the true king in Israel isn't the one with the most power but the one most shaped by God's word. Leadership in God's kingdom is self-emptying, grounded in the awareness that authority is stewardship, not ownership.

Spiritually, this passage calls us to examine how we wield influence, whether in families, churches, workplaces, or communities. Power reveals the heart. It shows whether we serve or dominate, whether we seek truth or protect ourselves, whether we build community or fortify ego. God invites us into a different kind of leadership: humble, accountable, truth-centered, grounded in prayerful dependence.

This text also challenges us to resist the idols that distort justice. When we chase security, success, or approval as ultimate things, we bend truth to protect them. But when God alone holds our allegiance, the heart becomes free to speak honestly, act justly, and love boldly.

And in Jesus, this entire chapter bursts into fullness. He's the just judge who defends the vulnerable. He's the faithful priest who teaches truth without corruption. He's the humble King who refuses violence, refuses privilege, refuses self-exaltation. He writes God's law not on scrolls, but in his very life. Through his Spirit, he writes laws on our hearts. In Christ, justice and mercy embrace. In him, leadership becomes servanthood. In him, truth becomes liberation.

Guiding Truth: Let God's justice and humility shape how you lead, love, and live: power becomes life-giving only when surrendered to truth.

Reflection: How do I handle influence, small or large, and where might God be inviting me into more profound humility or truthfulness? What idols or fears might be tempting me to bend justice, avoid truth, or protect myself rather than serve others?

Prayer: God of justice and mercy, shape my heart in truth. Remove pride, fear, and self-protection. Teach me to lead with humility, to discern with wisdom, and to act with compassion. Let my life reflect your justice and my decisions reveal your love. Form in me the character of your true King. Amen.

Day 29: Listening for the Voice That Leads to Life

Reading: Deuteronomy 18:1–22

Moses continues to shape Israel into a people whose lives reflect the character of God. In this chapter, the focus turns to who they listen to. Israel is surrounded by nations that rely on divination, sorcery, omens, and attempts to manipulate the unseen. These practices promise knowledge and control, but they distort the heart and enslave the imagination. God wants something entirely different for Israel: a life built on trust, not fear; revelation, not manipulation; covenant, not control.

The Levites, who receive no inherited land, are sustained by the offerings of the people. This arrangement is sacred and theological. Their portion is God. Their vocation is presence, teaching, prayer, and discernment. They embody dependence, reminding the whole community that life is grounded in gift rather than grasping.

Moses warns the people to avoid every form of occult practice, because these practices attempt to gain power over mysteries that belong to God alone. They short-circuit trust. They turn spirituality into technique. They deform the heart by making fear the engine of decision-making. God wants Israel to walk in freedom, not in the shadow of anxious control.

Then comes one of the most hopeful promises in the Old Testament: "The Lord your God will raise for you a prophet . . . You must listen to this prophet." God will speak, not through dark arts or coercive rituals but through chosen messengers who bear the divine word with clarity, truth, and compassion. These prophets will reveal the heart of God.

Moses recalls Israel's fear at Sinai, when they trembled at God's voice and begged for a mediator. God honors that request: prophets will speak on God's behalf. True prophets will call the people back to covenant, truth, justice, and mercy. False prophets (those who speak in God's name without God's authority) are dangerous because they lead hearts astray and wound communities. Discernment becomes a spiritual necessity.

Spiritually, this passage confronts us with a crucial question: *Whose voice is shaping my life?* In a world overflowing with noise (political rhetoric, cultural pressure, religious performance, self-help mantras, inner fear), Moses urges us to listen for the voice that leads to life. Not every impressive voice is trustworthy. Not every confident message is valid. Not every spiritual-sounding word carries the breath of God.

This chapter invites us to cultivate holy attentiveness, and to learn to recognize God's voice by its fruit: clarity, not confusion; peace, not fear; justice, not exploitation; mercy, not manipulation. When God speaks, the heart is widened, humbled, healed, and reoriented toward love.

And in Jesus, this promise is fulfilled in radiant fullness. He is the prophet like Moses, yet greater. He speaks not merely about God but as God. His words set free. His authority is compassionate. His truth restores. To listen to him is to find the path that leads through wilderness into life.

This passage calls us to resist the voices that twist truth, the habits that dull discernment, and the fears that seek control. It urges us to seek the One whose voice brings freedom, wisdom, and peace.

Guiding Truth: Listen for God's authentic voice; let it shape your choices, calm your fears, and lead you into life.

Reflection: What voices, internal or external, most shape my decisions, and how do they align with the character of God? How can I cultivate a more profound attentiveness to the voice of Jesus in Scripture, prayer, and community?

Prayer: God of truth, quiet the noise within and around me. Teach me to discern your voice and follow where you lead. Turn my heart from fear and false guidance, and anchor me in your wisdom, compassion, and peace. Let your words shape my life. Amen.

Day 30: Building a Community Where Justice Protects Life

Reading: Deuteronomy 19:1–21

As Israel prepares to inhabit the land, Moses turns again to the shape of justice. This chapter is tender and fierce at once: tender toward the vulnerable, fierce toward anything that distorts truth. God desires a community where life is protected, truth is honored, and justice is carried out with compassion and integrity.

First, Moses commands the establishment of cities of refuge, places where someone who has accidentally taken a life can flee for safety until a fair hearing can take place. This is remarkable in the ancient world. God refuses to let vengeance dictate justice. God protects the one at risk of retaliation, insisting that fear, grief, or rage mustn't override truth. The cities of refuge embody God's heart: mercy displayed in justice, protection offered before judgment.

This practice reveals something fundamental about God's character. Justice is protective. It seeks to preserve life, not simply to punish wrongdoing. It honors complexity, refuses quick assumptions, and insists that every person (even the one implicated in tragedy) deserves compassion, due process, and dignity.

Next, Moses addresses the moving of boundary markers, an act that seems small but is profoundly unjust. Shifting a property line steals livelihood, land, identity, and inheritance. God cares about these "small" acts of injustice because they reveal what lives in the heart: greed, disregard, and exploitation. In God's kingdom, justice includes the unseen, the subtle, the easily hidden.

Then Moses turns to the matter of witnesses and false testimony. A single witness is never enough. Truth must be established through careful discernment. And if a witness lies (trying to harm another with false accusation), that deceit is considered violence. False testimony destroys trust and community. God commands that the harm intended by the false witness be returned upon them, to preserve the integrity of justice.

Spiritually, this chapter weighs heavily on us. It invites us to examine our impulses toward quick judgment, our assumptions about others, our careless words that may harm reputations, and the ways we let anger or fear shape our sense of justice. God calls us to be people who protect life first, who listen, discern, and refuse to rush toward conclusions that may destroy rather than heal.

This passage also calls us to guard the "boundary markers" in our own lives: honesty, integrity, compassion, and humility. These boundaries are easily shifted when self-interest rises. God invites us to anchor ourselves in practices that honor truth, protect the vulnerable, and cultivate a community of deep trust.

And this chapter points us to Jesus. He becomes our city of refuge, the One we flee to when we're guilty, afraid, broken, or misunderstood. In him, justice and mercy embrace. He exposes false accusations, defends the vulnerable, and protects life even at the cost of his own. His cross reveals the seriousness of both sin and grace; his resurrection assures us that no injustice has the last word.

In following him, we become people who seek justice out of love, people who defend truth, protect the vulnerable, and create spaces where life can flourish.

Guiding Truth: Let justice in your life protect the vulnerable, honor truth, and reflect the mercy that has sheltered you.

Reflection: Where am I tempted to judge quickly rather than listen carefully and protect life? How can I become a "refuge" for others, someone who offers safety, truthfulness, and compassion?

Prayer: God of justice and mercy, teach me to protect life with tenderness and pursue truth with humility. Guard my heart from quick judgment and false assumptions. Make me a refuge for others, reflecting your compassion, courage, and steadfast love in all I do. Amen.

Day 31: Courage Shaped by Trust, Not Fear

Reading: Deuteronomy 20:1–20

Moses addresses Israel as they prepare to face conflict: armies larger, weapons stronger, and odds stacked against them. The first words spoken into this moment are words of reassurance: "Don't be afraid." Israel is reminded that victory doesn't rest on numbers or force, but on the faithful presence of the God who brought them out of bondage. Courage here is trust grounded in memory.

Before any battle begins, the priest speaks to steady hearts. This detail matters. War is acknowledged as costly, frightening, and disruptive. God's concern is the preservation of a people shaped by covenant rather than fear. Even in conflict, God calls Israel to remember who they are and whose they are.

Then come the exemptions: those newly married, those who have planted vineyards or built homes, those whose hearts tremble with fear are sent home. This is astonishing. God values human life and emotional honesty more than military efficiency. Fear is acknowledged. Fragile joy is protected. Life is honored even in the shadow of conflict. The message is clear: the goal is faithfulness shaped by compassion.

Moses also distinguishes wars of preservation and acts of destruction. Israel is instructed to seek peace where possible, to offer terms before violence. Even when conflict is unavoidable, restraint is commanded. Fruit trees aren't to be destroyed. Life-sustaining resources are to be protected. This insistence reveals God's deep concern for creation and future generations. Violence must never become indiscriminate. Power must always be bounded by responsibility.

Spiritually, this passage speaks to the inner battles we face, the conflicts that arise when fear threatens to dominate our decisions. Many of us fight wars within: anxiety against trust, resentment against forgiveness, self-protection against love. God's word to us is the same: don't be afraid. Not because the struggle is imaginary, but because we aren't alone in it. God offers presence.

This chapter also reshapes how Christians live in a violent world. It calls us to resist glorifying power, to honor vulnerability, to seek peace where possible, and to practice restraint even when we feel justified. It invites us to build communities that protect life, tell the truth about fear, and refuse to sacrifice humanity for the sake of winning.

In Jesus, this vision is transformed and fulfilled. He confronts evil without mirroring it. He refuses coercive power and chooses the way of sacrificial love. His courage is rooted in love and trust. He faces the cross without fear because he entrusts himself wholly to God. Following him means engaging conflict differently, fighting injustice without hatred, resisting evil without losing compassion, choosing love even when it costs deeply.

Deuteronomy 20 doesn't teach us to love war. It teaches us to love life more than victory, trust more than fear, and God more than our own strength.

Guiding Truth: Face every battle, inner or outer, anchored in trust, protecting life, and refusing to let fear rule your heart.

Reflection: What fears currently shape my decisions, and how might trust in God's presence reshape my courage? Where am I being called to seek peace, practice restraint, or protect life rather than "win"?

Prayer: Faithful God, when fear rises and conflict looms, steady my heart in your presence. Teach me courage rooted in trust, restraint shaped by compassion, and strength guided by love. Guard my life from fear's rule, and form me into a witness of peace in a fractured world. Amen.

Day 32: Bearing Responsibility, Honoring Dignity

Reading: Deuteronomy 21:1–23

This chapter gathers a series of laws that may feel fragmented, yet they share a single moral gravity: human life matters, even when situations are broken, complex, or unresolved. Moses is teaching Israel how to live when things aren't ideal, when guilt is unclear, relationships are strained, power is uneven, or justice feels costly. Faithfulness, here, isn't abstract; it's practiced in the mess.

The chapter opens with an unsolved murder. Rather than ignoring it, the community must take responsibility. Elders gather, a ritual of atonement is enacted, and the people publicly confess their dependence on mercy. Even when no culprit can be named, life lost still matters. Violence is never shrugged off as unfortunate. The community bears collective grief and seeks cleansing. God refuses to let death become normal.

Then come laws that protect vulnerable women captured in war. In a violent ancient world, this instruction is quietly radical. A woman isn't to be treated as spoil but as a person with grief, dignity, and time. Power is restrained. Desire is slowed. Human worth is safeguarded. God bends the law toward mercy in a context already shaped by brokenness.

The chapter continues with inheritance laws protecting a firstborn child who might otherwise be displaced by favoritism. Justice here isn't about affection but about fairness. God guards against the quiet injustices that grow inside families, the ones justified by love but rooted in self-interest.

Then comes the hard word about a persistently rebellious child. This text isn't a license for cruelty but a sobering acknowledgment that communal life has limits. It names the tragic truth that unchecked violence corrodes the whole community. Yet even here, the responsibility lies with the community, not private vengeance. Justice is public, restrained, and grave.

Finally, the chapter ends with a striking instruction: a body mustn't be left hanging overnight. Even someone executed for wrongdoing mustn't be treated with contempt. Death doesn't erase dignity. Shame isn't meant to linger. The land itself is protected from defilement by cruelty.

Spiritually, this chapter presses us to ask how we treat life when it's inconvenient, ambiguous, or complex. Do we rush past suffering we can't explain? Do we justify harshness because it feels deserved? Do we protect our own comfort at the expense of another's dignity? God calls us to something better, to take responsibility where we can, restrain power where it tempts us, and honor humanity even in failure.

This passage finds its most profound meaning in Jesus. He bears responsibility for the violence he did not commit. He is treated as cursed, hung publicly, shamed beyond measure, and yet even in death, his body is handled with care. He absorbs the curse so others can be restored. In him, justice and mercy meet without denial or despair.

To follow him is to become people who refuse indifference, who protect dignity, who take responsibility for the world we share, and who trust that mercy is never wasted, even when situations are unresolved.

Guiding Truth: Honor human dignity in every circumstance, take responsibility, restrain power, and let mercy shape your response to brokenness.

Reflection: Where am I tempted to detach from responsibility because a situation feels too complex or uncomfortable? How might God be calling me to protect dignity, especially when failure, shame, or ambiguity are present?

Prayer: God of justice and compassion, teach me to honor life where it's fragile and dignity where it's threatened. Guard my heart from indifference and cruelty. Shape my responses with mercy, restraint, and courage, that my life may reflect your care for every person. Amen.

Day 33: Faithfulness in the Small and the Sacred

Reading: Deuteronomy 22:1–30

This chapter gathers a series of laws that seem ordinary, even mundane: lost animals, fallen donkeys, boundary markers, clothing, birds' nests. And then it turns toward matters that feel deeply personal and painful: sexuality, power, faithfulness, and violation. The movement is deliberate. Moses is teaching Israel that covenant faithfulness reaches into the smallest details and the most vulnerable places of human life.

The opening instructions are striking in their simplicity: if you see a neighbor's animal straying or burdened, you mustn't look away. You must help. Faithfulness begins with attention. Love takes shape in interruption. God is forming a people who refuse indifference, who notice what's lost, who bear one another's burdens, who take responsibility for the wellbeing of others even when it costs time or effort.

These small acts of care reveal a larger truth: what we ignore slowly shapes who we become. To pass by what's inconvenient is to train the heart toward hardness. To stop and help is to become a person capable of compassion. Covenant life is practiced in these moments where no applause follows.

The chapter's middle section continues this theme of restraint and care. God places limits on human power, even over animals and nature. Don't take both a mother bird and its young. Life is to be handled with reverence, not exploitation. Possession never justifies cruelty. Power is always accountable to mercy.

Then the chapter turns toward matters of sexual integrity, consent, and truthfulness, texts that must be read with seriousness and sorrow. In an ancient world where women were often treated as property, these laws insist that sexual violence isn't a private matter but a communal injustice. Violation is named as violence. Deceit is exposed. Responsibility is demanded. Though rooted in an ancient context, the heart of these commands is clear: God stands against abuse, coercion, and exploitation. Sexual faithfulness is about honoring the dignity of another's body and story.

Spiritually, this chapter presses us to examine how we handle power, subtle or overt. Do I protect the vulnerable or protect myself? Do I tell the truth even when it costs my reputation? Do I treat bodies, relationships, and trust as sacred, or as tools for my own desire? God's concern here is the preservation of dignity.

This passage also invites us to take responsibility for the spaces we inhabit. To build parapets on rooftops is to anticipate harm and prevent it. Faithfulness doesn't only respond to crisis; it plans for care. Love thinks ahead. Justice asks not only, "What did I do wrong?" but "What could I do to protect others?"

And in Jesus, the heart of this chapter comes into focus. He notices the overlooked, restores the violated, and confronts those who misuse power. He embodies a holiness that protects rather than shames, that heals rather than exploits. He teaches us that faithfulness is lived in daily choices to love attentively, truthfully, and sacrificially.

Deuteronomy 22 calls us into a way of life where nothing is too small for care and nothing too sacred for reverence.

Guiding Truth: Practice faithfulness in every detail: attention, restraint, and care are the soil where love grows.

Reflection: Where might God be inviting me to practice attentiveness rather than indifference in my daily life? How do I use power (relational, emotional, or social) and how can it better reflect dignity and care?

Prayer: God of compassion and truth, shape my heart in the small moments and the sacred ones. Teach me to notice, to protect, and to honor dignity wherever it's fragile. Guard me from indifference and misuse of power, and form my life as an offering of faithful love. Amen.

Day 34: Holiness That Makes Room for Mercy

Reading: Deuteronomy 23:1–25

This chapter gathers laws about belonging, purity, community boundaries, and everyday ethics. At first glance, it can feel like a tightening of exclusion: rules about who may enter the assembly, how the camp must remain clean, how debts and vows are handled. But beneath these instructions runs a deeper current: God is shaping a community whose holiness protects life, honors dignity, and makes space for mercy.

Moses speaks first about who may enter the assembly. These rules reflect Israel's fragile formation in a violent ancient world. They're statements about safeguarding a community learning to live differently, free from the exploitation, ritual violence, and coercion that once enslaved them. Holiness here is about preserving a people from patterns that would undo them before they're ready to bear the weight of freedom.

Yet even as boundaries are named, mercy presses in. Israel is told not to despise Edomites or Egyptians (former enemies and oppressors) because history is complicated and grace refuses simple enemies. Time and generations matter. Healing is possible. God's covenant imagination moves toward reconciliation rather than permanent exclusion.

The chapter then turns to the holiness of the camp itself. God is described as walking among the tents. Because divine presence dwells with them, even bodily practices matter. This is reverence. God cares about embodied life. Bodies are places where holiness is practiced. Everyday actions (how we treat our bodies, our environment, our shared spaces) become acts of respect toward the God who chooses to dwell among ordinary people.

Then comes a striking command: escaped enslaved people aren't to be returned to their masters. In a world where slavery was assumed, this instruction is revolutionary. God sides with the vulnerable. Refuge is honored over property. Safety matters more than economic convenience. This single verse exposes the heart of God, a God who breaks chains and refuses to cooperate with oppression.

Moses also addresses economic ethics: charging interest to people experiencing poverty is forbidden, vows are to be kept with integrity, and generosity toward neighbors is encouraged. You may eat from a neighbor's vineyard, but not exploit it. Need is honored; greed is restrained. God is forming a people whose economy reflects trust rather than fear, sufficiency rather than hoarding.

Spiritually, this chapter challenges our instincts around belonging and boundaries. Holiness is about keeping love intact. Boundaries exist to protect what is fragile, not to justify contempt. The test of holiness is how we protect the vulnerable, tell the truth, honor our word, and practice restraint with power.

In Jesus, the trajectory of this chapter becomes unmistakable. He welcomes those once excluded, honors bodies, shelters the vulnerable, and calls his followers into a holiness that heals rather than harms. He fulfills holiness, revealing that the deepest purity is love practiced with courage and compassion.

Deuteronomy 23 invites us into a holiness spacious enough for mercy, sturdy enough for truth, and grounded enough to protect life wherever it is fragile.

Guiding Truth: Live a holiness that protects the vulnerable, honors dignity, and keeps mercy at the center of community life.

Reflection: Where might my understanding of holiness need to be reshaped by compassion and justice? How can I practice integrity and generosity in ordinary, embodied ways this week?

Prayer: God who dwells among us, shape my life into a space where your presence is honored. Guard me from hardness of heart. Teach me a holiness that shelters the vulnerable, tells the truth, and lives with mercy at its core. Let my faith make room for love. Amen.

Day 35: Justice for the Poor and Marginalized

Reading: Deuteronomy 24:1–22

Moses gathers a collection of laws that, on the surface, might seem unconnected: regulations about divorce and remarriage, pledges and wages, legal testimony, and gleaning rights in the fields. Yet beneath this apparent fragmentation pulses a singular heartbeat: the protection of human dignity, especially among those most vulnerable to being overlooked, exploited, or forgotten. God is teaching Israel that holiness isn't merely cultic or ceremonial, it's woven into the fabric of economic relationships, family structures, employment practices, and the rhythms of harvest.

The opening verses address the painful complexity of broken marriages. The regulations don't endorse divorce; they restrain its cruelty. In a world where women held almost no legal standing, these laws create breathing room for dignity. A certificate of divorce provides legal protection, proof that a woman is free to remarry, not discarded into social oblivion. Even amid brokenness, God carves out pathways of mercy.

Then Moses turns to the newlyweds. A man who has just taken a spouse shouldn't be sent to war or burdened with heavy obligations for a year. Joy is to be protected. Love needs space to root. In a culture built on productivity and duty, this command whispers something countercultural: relationships matter more than efficiency. The formation of a household is sacred work, and God guards it against the relentless demands of empire-building.

The laws about pledges and wages reveal God's fierce concern for economic justice. You must not take a millstone as security; that would be taking someone's livelihood, their very means of survival. A cloak taken as collateral must be returned before nightfall, because the person experiencing poverty has nothing else to sleep in. Workers must be paid at the end of each day, because delayed wages can mean hunger for families living on the edge. These aren't suggestions; they're divine commands that reveal the character of a God who hears the cries of the exploited.

The command about legal testimony reaches toward something deeper still: no one should be punished for the crimes of another. Each person bears responsibility for their own actions. This principle pushes back against systems that punish entire families or communities for individual offences. Justice, in God's economy, is precise, protecting the innocent from collective vengeance.

And then comes the refrain that echoes through these verses like a drum: "Remember that you were slaves in Egypt." This is the moral center. Israel's entire ethical imagination is grounded in memory. You know what it feels like to be powerless, forgotten, and exploited. You know the ache of injustice. Let that memory reshape how you treat the foreigner, the orphan, the widow, the worker who depends on your integrity. Justice flows from remembrance. Compassion grows from identifying with those who suffer.

The chapter closes with laws about gleaning: leaving the edges of fields unharvested, not going back to retrieve a forgotten sheaf or shake every olive from the tree. These provisions create space for the hungry to feed themselves with dignity. Charity here isn't humiliating handouts but participation in the harvest. People with low incomes aren't beggars; they're workers gleaning what remains. Generosity is built into the system, not as an afterthought but as a structural commitment to shared flourishing.

Spiritually, this passage searches me. Where have I prioritized efficiency over relationship? Where have my economic practices (how I spend, save, pay, withhold) failed to account for the vulnerable? Where has forgetfulness eroded my compassion? These laws press gently but firmly against the comfortable assumptions that let injustice hide in plain sight.

Following Christ means embodying this same attentiveness. Jesus stands squarely in this tradition when he announces good news to those experiencing poverty, touches the untouchable, and sees the overlooked. His kingdom is one where the last are first, where dignity is restored, where the hungry are filled, and the powerful are sent away empty. To follow him is to let these ancient commands reshape our imaginations, to build communities where no one is invisible, where justice and mercy are the air we breathe, where memory of our own deliverance births compassion for all who still wait for freedom.

Guiding Truth: Let the memory of grace received become the engine of justice extended: see the overlooked, protect the vulnerable, and leave room for others to flourish.

Reflection: Where might my daily practices (economic, relational, or vocational) be inadvertently harming those with less power than I have? How can I build "gleaning spaces" into my life, margins of generosity that allow others to participate in flourishing with dignity?

Prayer: God of justice and mercy, open my eyes to those I've failed to see. Let the memory of your grace reshape how I treat the vulnerable. Teach me to build structures of generosity into my life, that others might flourish. Make my hands instruments of your compassion, my resources tools of your justice, and my heart a reflection of your fierce love for all who are forgotten. Amen.

Day 36: Fairness, Integrity, and Restorative Justice

Reading: Deuteronomy 25:1–19

This chapter gathers laws that seem, at first glance, disconnected: limits on corporal punishment, the muzzling of oxen, levirate marriage, a strange case of immodest intervention, honest weights and measures, and the command to remember Amalek. Yet beneath this apparent fragmentation lies a unified vision, a community where dignity is protected, justice is tempered by mercy, and memory shapes moral action.

The opening verses address punishment. When someone is found guilty, the penalty must fit the offence and have limits. Forty lashes, no more. Why? "So that your neighbor isn't degraded in your eyes." Even the guilty retain dignity. Punishment here is about restoration within bounds. The moment we strip another person of their humanity, even someone who has done wrong, we lose something of our own. Justice that degrades the punished eventually degrades the punisher.

Then comes a law that feels almost whimsical: don't muzzle an ox while it treads grain. Let the animal eat from the labor it performs. This is a window into God's character. If even working animals deserve to share in the fruit of their effort, how much more do human workers deserve fair treatment? The apostle Paul saw this and applied it to those who labor in ministry and service. Generosity toward those who work for us is justice.

The laws about levirate marriage address a different vulnerability: the widow without children, facing social erasure in a world where family continuity meant survival. A brother-in-law is called to raise up offspring for the deceased, ensuring the family name endures, and the widow isn't abandoned. When someone refuses this duty, the ritual of the sandal and public shaming are accountability measures. The community names the failure to care for the vulnerable. Covenant life means we can't simply opt out of responsibility when it becomes inconvenient.

The brief law about a woman intervening in a fight by seizing a man's genitals feels jarring to modern readers. Yet the underlying principle is restraint: even in defense of a loved one, there are limits. Proportionality matters. Violence that exceeds necessity, that aims to shame or permanently harm, crosses a line. Justice isn't served by escalation.

Then Moses turns to commerce: honest weights and measures. This law exposes how injustice hides in plain sight. A merchant with two sets of stones, one for buying, one for selling, slowly bleeds the community through countless small deceptions. God calls this an abomination. Not murder, not idolatry, but cheating in the marketplace. Integrity in the ordinary transactions of daily life reveals what we actually believe about God and neighbor. Small dishonesties erode trust, and without trust, community collapses.

The chapter closes with a command to remember Amalek, the nation that attacked Israel's weakest and most vulnerable as they fled Egypt. This is a call to perpetual moral vigilance. There are forces in the world that prey on the defenseless, and God's people must never forget that such predation exists. Remembering Amalek means refusing to become Amalek: refusing to exploit weakness, refusing to attack those who lag, refusing to let power become cruelty.

Spiritually, this passage searches me. Where have I degraded others in the name of justice? Where have I muzzled those who labor for my benefit? Where have small dishonesties crept into my dealings? Where have I abandoned the vulnerable because responsibility felt burdensome? These laws are mirrors.

And in Jesus, this entire chapter finds its fulfilment. He's the one who bears punishment without losing dignity, and who restores dignity to those the world discards. He's the one who sees the widow, the worker, the cheated, the forgotten. He refuses to prey on weakness; instead, he lays down power for the sake of the vulnerable. To follow him is to build communities where justice never forgets mercy, where integrity governs the smallest transactions, and where the defenseless find protection rather than exploitation.

Guiding Truth: Let integrity shape your smallest dealings and mercy temper your pursuit of justice, for how we treat the vulnerable reveals who we truly are.

Reflection: Where might small dishonesties or quiet neglect be eroding my integrity and harming others? How can I better protect the dignity of those who are vulnerable, punished, or easily overlooked in my community?

Prayer: God of justice and mercy, search my heart. Expose the places where I've degraded others or let dishonesty creep into my dealings. Teach me to protect the vulnerable, to deal fairly, and to remember that every person bears your image. Shape my life into a witness of your restoring love. Amen.

Day 37: Offering First fruits and Confession of Faith

Reading: Deuteronomy 26:1–19

This chapter is one of the most beautiful in Deuteronomy. It gathers the entire story of Israel (wandering, slavery, deliverance, and gift) into a single liturgical act. Moses instructs the people that when they finally enter the land and harvest its fruit, they're to take the first fruits of the soil, place them in a basket, and bring them before God. And as they present their offering, they're to speak. Not silently. Not privately. But aloud, in words that rehearse the whole arc of grace.

The confession begins in vulnerability: "My ancestor was a wandering Aramean." This is Jacob: rootless, fleeing, uncertain. The story doesn't start with triumph but with displacement. Israel's identity is grounded in fragility. They went down to Egypt, few in number, and became a nation there, but also became enslaved. They cried out, and God heard. God saw affliction, toil, and oppression, and acted. With a mighty hand and outstretched arm, God brought them out, led them through, and gave them this land flowing with milk and honey.

This confession is astonishing in its honesty. It refuses to sanitize the past or inflate the present. It holds suffering and deliverance together without flinching. And it locates the worshipper firmly within a story that began long before their birth and will continue long after. To offer first fruits is to say: I'm not self-made. Everything I have flows from a grace

I didn't earn. The basket in my hands is evidence of a faithfulness that precedes me.

The act of bringing first fruits (not leftovers, not surplus, but the first and best) reorders desire. It trains the heart to hold abundance loosely. Gratitude becomes embodied, not merely felt. And the offering is presented before the priest, before the community, before God. Worship here is public testimony. It says to everyone watching: this is who God is, this is what God has done, and this is why I give.

Then Moses adds another instruction. Every third year, when the tithe is set aside for the Levite, the foreigner, the orphan, and the widow, the giver must make a second declaration: "I've removed the sacred portion from my house and given it to those you commanded." This is accountability. It's a confession that generosity has actually happened, that the vulnerable have been fed, that the community has been cared for, that obedience has moved from intention to action.

The chapter closes with covenant affirmation. God declares that Israel is a treasured possession. Israel declares God to be their God. The relationship is mutual, personal, and binding. Identity and belonging are sealed in this exchange. To be God's people is about being claimed by a love that chose the wandering, heard the crying, and led the enslaved into freedom.

Spiritually, this passage searches me with gentle force. Do I remember the story that holds me? Do I recognize that everything I have is a gift? Or have I slowly drifted into the illusion that my achievements are self-generated, my security self-made? The first fruits ritual is an antidote to amnesia. It anchors identity in grace rather than accomplishment. And it connects private blessing to public responsibility; the tithe for the vulnerable ensures that abundance never terminates on the one who receives it.

For those who follow Jesus, this chapter resonates with even more profound meaning. We, too, were wanderers: alienated, lost, enslaved to forces we couldn't overcome. We, too, cried out and were heard. In Christ, God's mighty hand reached into our bondage and brought us into a land of promise we did not earn. Every act of worship becomes an echo of this confession: I was lost, and I was found. I was dead, and I'm alive. The first fruits I offer are simply returning to the Giver what was always already a gift.

And if we've been so loved, then generosity toward the vulnerable is the shape gratitude takes when it matures. We give because we have received. We care for the foreigner, the orphan, the widow, because we remember what it was to wander, to be powerless, to need deliverance. The gospel doesn't end with personal salvation; it overflows into a community where no one is forgotten, and everyone belongs.

Guiding Truth: Remember the story that holds you: let gratitude for grace received reshape how you give, worship, and care for those in need.

Reflection: What story do I tell myself about how I got where I am, and does it make room for grace, vulnerability, and God's deliverance? How might offering my "first fruits" (time, resources, attention) reshape my relationship with abundance and my responsibility toward the vulnerable?

Prayer: Faithful God, I was wandering, and you found me. I was enslaved, and you set me free. Teach me to hold all I have as a gift. Let gratitude reshape my giving, my worship, and my care for those in need. Anchor my identity in your grace, and let my life become an offering of thanks. Amen.

Day 38: Covenant Renewal on Mounts Ebal and Gerizim

Reading: Deuteronomy 27:1–26

Moses knows he won't cross the Jordan. So he does what every faithful leader must eventually do: he prepares the people to continue without him. This chapter is a blueprint for what Israel must do the moment it enters the land. They're to set up large stones, coat them with plaster, and inscribe on them all the words of the law. Then they're to build an altar of uncut stones, no iron tool touching them, and offer sacrifices of peace and thanksgiving. The law is to be visible, public, and permanent. It's not hidden wisdom for elites but a word written where everyone can see.

The setting matters. Mount Ebal and Mount Gerizim stand opposite each other like two possibilities, two futures. The tribes will be divided between them: half on the mountain of blessing, half on the mountain of curse. And the Levites will stand in the valley and cry out the curses, each one met with the people's unified response: 'Amen.' This is covenant renewal as embodied drama. Israel isn't merely hearing the law; they're physically enacting choice, positioning their bodies in a landscape that speaks of consequence.

The twelve curses that follow are sobering. They target sins that hide: idolatry practiced in secret, dishonor of parents, moving a neighbor's boundary marker, misleading the blind, perverting justice for the vulnerable, sexual violations within the family, violence done in the dark, bribery that corrupts the courts. These aren't the loud, public sins that communities easily condemn. They're the quiet betrayals, the sins committed when no one is watching, the injustices that fester in hidden places.

And that's precisely the point. God sees what is hidden. The covenant community can't be built on external conformity alone. Integrity must reach into the unseen corners of life, into the home, the heart, the transactions no one audits. The curses expose the gap between public reputation and private reality. They press the question: Who am I when no one is looking? What would be revealed if the walls became transparent?

The people's "Amen" isn't passive agreement. It's ownership. It's saying, "Yes, I understand." Yes, I accept. Yes, I bind myself to this standard, knowing the weight of what I'm affirming. Covenant life requires conscious consent. No one drifts into faithfulness. We must choose, again and again, to align our hidden lives with our spoken commitments.

Spiritually, this passage confronts me with uncomfortable honesty. I'm often more concerned with how I appear than with who I actually am. I manage impressions. I curate a self for public consumption while neglecting the disordered loyalties and quiet compromises that shape my interior world. The curses of Deuteronomy 27 refuse to let me hide. They drag the secret into the light and ask: Will you say 'Amen' to a standard that searches you this deeply?

Yet even here, grace flickers. The altar built on Ebal, the mountain of curse, is an altar of peace offerings. Sacrifice stands in the place of judgment. Worship rises from the very ground associated with failure and consequence. This isn't a covenant of despair but of sober hope. God knows we'll fall short. God provides a way back.

And for those who follow Jesus, this chapter points forward to the one who stood under every curse we deserved. Paul writes that Christ became a curse for us, bearing the weight of the law's judgment so that blessing might flow to all who trust in him. The 'Amen' we now speak isn't dread but gratitude, not the desperate hope that we might measure up, but the quiet confidence that someone already has on our behalf. The hidden sins that would condemn us have been exposed, named, and absorbed by a love stronger than death.

This doesn't make integrity optional. It makes it possible. Freed from the terror of condemnation, we can finally be honest about who we are. We can bring the hidden into the light, not to earn acceptance but because we have already received it. The goal of the spiritual life isn't performance but transparency, a slow, grace-empowered alignment of the secret self with the God who sees all and loves still.

Guiding Truth: Bring your hidden life into the light. Integrity means becoming the same person in secret that you appear to be in public.

Reflection: What sins or compromises in my life remain hidden, and what would it mean to bring them into the light before God? How does knowing that Christ bore the curse for me change how I approach my own failures and the call to integrity?

Prayer: Searching God, you see what I hide from others and even from myself. Expose the secret places where sin has taken root. Free me from the exhausting work of impression management, and form in me an integrity that needs no audience. Thank you for the one who bore my curse. Let that grace make me whole. Amen.

Day 39: Blessings for Obedience

Reading: Deuteronomy 28:1–14

Moses opens this chapter with a cascade of blessings so lavish that it almost overwhelms. If Israel fully obeys, if they carefully follow all God's commands, then blessing will pursue them, in the city and in the country, in the womb and in the field, in the basket and in the kneading trough: blessing when they come in, blessing when they go out. Enemies who rise against them will be defeated. Rain will fall in season. The nation will lend, not borrow; it'll be the head, not the tail. The language is extravagant, almost dizzying in its abundance.

This isn't the prosperity gospel. It's something older and more complex. Moses is describing the natural fruit of a community aligned with the grain of the universe. When a society practices justice, honors the vulnerable, worships the true God, and refuses idolatry, inevitable consequences follow. Trust builds. Cooperation flourishes. The land yields its produce because the people tend it with gratitude rather than greed. Blessing here is relational, covenantal, communal. It's not magic; it's the shape of a life lived in sync with God's design.

Yet even as the blessings pour forth, a quiet condition pulses beneath them: "if you fully obey." The repetition is intentional. Moses knows the human heart. He knows how quickly we drift, how easily we forget, how subtly we begin to imagine that the blessings are ours by right rather than by grace. The condition isn't arbitrary; it's the acknowledgment that blessing flows from a relationship. Cut the root, and the fruit withers. Turn from the source, and the stream dries up.

The promise that Israel will be 'set high above all the nations' isn't triumphalism. It's a vocation. Israel is blessed to bless. They're lifted up so that others might see what a community looks like when it's ordered by divine love. The nations will observe and wonder: What god is so near? What laws are so just? Israel's flourishing is meant to be a window into the character of God, an invitation extended to the watching world.

Spiritually, this passage stirs both longing and discomfort in me. I want the blessing. I like the flourishing, the fruitfulness, the sense that life is working. But I am less eager for the obedience that roots it. I want harvest without planting, fruit without pruning, abundance without the slow, daily work of alignment. These verses remind me that there is no shortcut. Blessing isn't a transaction; it's the overflow of a life surrendered to the One who gives all good things.

And yet, if I am honest, I also know that obedience doesn't always yield visible blessing, at least not in the ways I expect. The righteous suffer. The faithful struggle. The obedient sometimes face loss rather than abundance. This tension is real, and the rest of Scripture wrestles with it openly. Job, the Psalms, Ecclesiastes, and the prophets all press against any simplistic formula. Blessing is true, but it's not a vending machine. The relationship is real, but the timing and shape of flourishing remain in God's hands.

For followers of Jesus, this passage takes on a different hue. We know that the one who obeyed fully, who never turned to the right or left, did not receive earthly blessing but a cross. Jesus embodied perfect covenant faithfulness, and the result was suffering, rejection, and death. Yet through that death came resurrection, and through resurrection came blessing poured out on the whole world. The economy of blessing has been transformed. It now flows not through a single nation's obedience but through the faithfulness of one person, offered on behalf of all.

This means that the blessings we receive are no longer contingent on our perfect performance. They're gifts of grace, secured by Christ's obedience. We still pursue faithfulness, not to earn blessings but because we have already been blessed beyond measure. Obedience becomes a

111

response, not a requirement. It's the shape love takes when it has been loved first. And the flourishing we seek isn't primarily material but spiritual: the fruit of the Spirit, the peace that passes understanding, the joy that survives suffering, the love that endures.

Moses' vision of blessing remains true, but it has been deepened. The head and not the tail, the lender and not the borrower, these images now speak of a people who live from abundance rather than scarcity, who give rather than grasp, who lead by serving, who flourish by pouring themselves out. The blessing of Deuteronomy 28 finds its fulfilment in communities shaped by the self-giving love of Christ.

Guiding Truth: Receive blessing as a gift, pursue faithfulness as a response, and let your flourishing become an invitation for others to see the goodness of God.

Reflection: Where have I sought blessing without the slow work of faithful obedience? How might my life, my flourishing, my generosity, my peace, become a witness that draws others toward the God who gives all good things?

Prayer: Generous God, every good gift flows from your hand. Forgive me for grasping at blessing while resisting the obedience that roots it. Teach me to receive with gratitude, to follow with trust, and to let my life become a window into your goodness. May my flourishing serve your purposes and draw others to your love. Amen.

Day 40: Curses for Disobedience

Reading: Deuteronomy 28:15–68

This is one of the most harrowing passages in Scripture. Where the first fourteen verses sang of blessing, these fifty-three verses descend into a catalogue of devastation so thorough it leaves the reader breathless. Cursed in the city, cursed in the country. Cursed in the womb, cursed in the field. Plague, fever, inflammation, drought, blight, mildew, madness, blindness, and confusion of mind. Enemies triumphant. Children taken. Bodies unburied. The heavens are bronze, the earth is iron. A nation scattered to the ends of the world, finding no rest, trembling day and night, longing for death.

The sheer weight of it is crushing. Moses holds nothing back. He wants Israel to feel the gravity of the choice before them. Covenant isn't a casual arrangement. It's life and death, blessing and curse, flourishing and destruction. The God who liberates is also the God who holds accountable. Love that rescues is also love that refuses to pretend consequences don't exist.

Yet we must read carefully. These curses aren't arbitrary punishments imposed by a vindictive deity. They're, in large part, the natural unravelling of a community that has abandoned the source of its life. When a society turns from justice, injustice consumes it. When people chase idols, those idols eventually devour what they promised to protect. When trust in God is replaced by confidence in military power, political alliances, or economic exploitation, the structures built on those foundations collapse under their own weight. The curses describe what happens when the fabric of covenant life is torn, when the relationships that hold a community together fray and finally snap.

The siege imagery is particularly devastating. Moses describes conditions so desperate that parents consume their own children, that the most gentle and refined become savage in their hunger. This is prophetic realism. Moses knows what happens when cities fall, when empires crush rebellious vassals, when war reduces human beings to their most desperate instincts. He has seen what Pharaoh's Egypt was capable of. He knows what lies ahead if Israel follows the same path of arrogance and idolatry.

The passage reaches its nadir with exile. Israel will be scattered among the nations, will serve other gods of wood and stone, will become a byword and an object of horror. And then, the final wound: they'll be taken back to Egypt in ships, offered as enslaved people, and no one will buy them. The exodus reversed. Liberation undone. The people who were brought out with a mighty hand will return in chains, and even then, they'll find no value in the eyes of their captors. It's a portrait of complete and utter loss.

Spiritually, this passage terrifies me, and it should. It refuses to let me imagine that my choices don't matter, that God is indifferent to how I live, that grace means consequence-free existence. The curses are a mirror held up to the human capacity for self-destruction. They ask: What am I building my life on? What idols have I trusted to deliver what only God can give? What slow unravelling is already underway in the places where I've turned from the source of life?

Yet I can't stay in terror. The story doesn't end here. Even within Deuteronomy, chapter 30 will speak of restoration, of return, of a God who gathers the scattered and circumcises hearts. The curses are real, but they aren't the final word. They're meant to drive us toward repentance, not despair. They're the severe mercy of a God who would rather wound with truth than soothe with lies.

And for those who follow Jesus, this passage takes on yet another dimension. Paul writes that Christ became a curse for us, hanging on a tree to absorb the weight of the covenant's broken promises. Every devastation listed in Deuteronomy 28, the abandonment, the exile, the horror, the shame, was gathered up and carried by the one who had no sin. The curses were not cancelled by being ignored; they were exhausted by being borne. Jesus descended into the depths so that we might be lifted out.

This doesn't make the curses irrelevant. It makes them bearable. We can look at the worst of what disobedience produces, the unravelling, the exile, the loss, and know that even there, grace has already gone ahead of us. We can face the consequences of our choices with sorrow but not despair, because the one who bore the curse now offers restoration. The way back to blessing isn't through performance but through the open arms of the one who absorbed the curse and speaks peace.

Deuteronomy 28 is a passage to be read on our knees. It sobers us. It strips away presumption. But it also drives us toward the only refuge strong enough to hold us when everything else collapses: the faithful love of a God who enters our curse to bring us home.

Guiding Truth: Face the weight of your choices honestly, and then run to the one who bore the curse so that you might find your way home.

Reflection: What slow unravelling might be underway in my life because I've turned from God toward lesser sources of security or meaning? How does knowing that Christ bore the curse change how I approach my own failures and the call to return?

Prayer: Holy God, I tremble before the weight of this passage. Expose the idols I've trusted and the unravelling I've ignored. Thank you for the one who bore the curse I deserved. Lead me back from exile, restore what I've broken, and anchor my life in your faithful love. Amen.

Day 41: Remembering God's Mercy and Promise of Restoration

Reading: Deuteronomy 29:1–29

Moses gathers the people one final time. The curses have been spoken. The weight of consequence hangs in the air. And now, before the covenant is sealed, Moses does something pastors and prophets have always done: he tells the story again. He reminds them of Egypt, of the wilderness, of the clothes that did not wear out and the bread that fell from heaven. He rehearses the victories over Sihon and Og. He names what God has done, not so they'll feel nostalgic, but so they'll understand who they are dealing with.

Then comes one of the most haunting lines in Scripture: "But to this day the Lord has not given you a mind that understands or eyes that see or ears that hear." Israel witnessed the plagues, walked through the sea, ate manna for forty years, and still did not fully perceive. Revelation doesn't guarantee comprehension. Proximity to miracles doesn't automatically produce transformed hearts. There is a blindness that persists even in the presence of overwhelming evidence. And only God can open the eyes that see.

This is a lament. Moses grieves for a people who have been carried by grace and still struggle to trust. He knows them. He has led them for forty years. He has watched them complain, rebel, and turn back toward Egypt in their hearts even as their feet moved forward. And yet he doesn't abandon them. He keeps preaching, keeps reminding, keeps calling them into covenant. The pastoral heart refuses to give up even when the evidence suggests giving up would be reasonable.

The covenant ceremony that follows is radically inclusive. Moses addresses not only the leaders and elders but also the children, the women, the foreigners, the woodcutters, and the water carriers. Everyone stands before God. Everyone is included in the oath. Everyone bears responsibility. Covenant isn't a private transaction between God and spiritual elites; it's a communal commitment that binds the whole people, from the highest to the lowest, from those present to generations not yet born.

Moses then warns against the person who hears the covenant and secretly thinks, "I'll be safe, even though I persist in going my own way." This is the danger of presumption, the assumption that grace covers without transforming, that belonging to the community provides immunity from consequence. Moses names this self-deception as a root that produces bitter poison. One person's hidden rebellion can spread corruption throughout the whole. Private compromise has public consequences.

The chapter moves toward devastation. Moses describes a future generation standing amid the ruins, asking, "Why has the Lord done this to this land?" And the answer will be plain: "Because they abandoned the covenant." The smoking wasteland will be its own sermon. The nations will look and know. Disobedience writes its consequences into the landscape itself.

And then, in the final verse, Moses speaks words that have echoed through centuries of Jewish and Christian reflection: "The secret things belong to the Lord our God, but the things revealed belong to our children and to us forever, that we may follow all the words of this law." There is a mystery we can't penetrate. Some questions won't be answered this side of eternity. But what has been revealed is enough. We aren't called to master the hidden counsels of God; we're called to obey what has been made plain. Faithfulness doesn't require omniscience. It requires trust.

Spiritually, this passage searches me in multiple directions. I recognize myself in the people who witnessed wonders and still struggled to see. I know the temptation to presume upon grace, to imagine that my private compromises will have no consequence. I feel the weight of communal responsibility, that my faithfulness or unfaithfulness affects others. And I am humbled by the reminder that I don't need to understand everything; I need to obey what has been revealed.

For those who follow Jesus, this chapter resonates with both warning and hope. Jesus himself lamented over Jerusalem: "If you had only known what would bring you peace, but now it's hidden from your eyes." The blindness Moses named continued. And yet, in Christ, eyes are opened. The Spirit gives understanding that forty years of miracles could not produce. What the law could not accomplish, a heart that truly sees, grace makes possible.

The covenant we're invited into through Christ is still radically inclusive, every tribe, tongue, and nation gathered before God. It still requires honesty about our tendency toward self-deception. It still holds secrets and reveals them in tension. But now the covenant is written not on stone but on hearts, sealed not with the blood of animals but with the blood of the one who saw clearly, obeyed fully, and opened the way for all who would trust.

Guiding Truth: Release your grip on what is hidden and give yourself fully to what has been revealed. Faithful obedience doesn't require understanding everything.

Reflection: Where might I be presuming upon grace, imagining that my private compromises carry no consequence? What has God already revealed that I am resisting or delaying in obeying?

Prayer: God of revelation and mystery, open my eyes to see what you have shown. Forgive my presumption and my blindness. Free me from the need to understand everything before I obey anything. Anchor my life in what you have revealed, and teach me to trust you with what remains hidden. Amen.

Day 42: The Call to Choose Life

Reading: Deuteronomy 30:1–20

After the terror of the curses, after the sober warning of chapter 29, Moses does something unexpected. He speaks of return. He imagines Israel scattered among the nations, living in the very exile he has just described, and he says, even there, the story isn't over. "When you and your children return to the Lord your God and obey with all your heart and with all your soul . . . then the Lord your God will restore your fortunes and have compassion on you and gather you again."

This is breathtaking. The curses weren't the final word. Exile isn't permanent. The God who scatters also gathers. The God who wounds also heals. Even from the farthest corners of the earth, even after the worst unfaithfulness, the way home remains open. Moses doesn't minimize the consequences of disobedience, but he refuses to let consequences become destiny. Grace outlasts judgment. Mercy waits on the other side of ruin.

And then Moses speaks of something even more remarkable: "The Lord your God will circumcise your hearts and the hearts of your descendants, so that you may love the Lord your God with all your heart and with all your soul, and live." Here is the deepest promise of Deuteronomy. God will do what Israel couldn't do for themselves. The problem was never merely external, behavior to be corrected, rules to be followed. The problem was the heart itself, hardened, resistant, incapable of the love it was made for. And God promises to perform surgery on that heart, to cut away what blocks love, to make possible what the law alone could never produce.

This is grace before the word "grace" became a theological term. It's the recognition that human effort, however sincere, will always fall short. It's the promise that God doesn't simply command transformation; God accomplishes it. The circumcised heart isn't achieved; it's received. It's a gift all the way down.

Moses then insists that the command isn't too difficult, not too far away. It isn't in heaven, requiring someone to ascend and bring it down. It isn't across the sea, so an impossible journey isn't needed. "No, the word is very near you; it's in your mouth and in your heart so you may obey it." This is the intimacy of the covenant. God's will isn't hidden behind elaborate rituals or esoteric knowledge. It's accessible, speakable, and livable. The distance we feel from God isn't geographical; it's the distance of a turned heart. And that distance can be closed by turning back.

The chapter builds toward its climax with some of the most famous words in the Old Testament: "I've set before you life and death, blessings and curses. Now choose life, so that you and your children may live." The choice is real. The options are stark. Moses doesn't pretend neutrality is possible. To drift is already to choose. To delay is already to decide. The summons is urgent because the stakes are ultimate.

And what does choosing life look like? Moses names it: "Love the Lord your God, listen to his voice, and hold fast to him. For the Lord is your life." Life is the relationship itself. To be connected to the source of all being is to live. To be severed from that source is death, no matter how much activity continues. The choice before Israel, and before us, isn't merely moral. It's existential. It's about where we locate our lives.

Spiritually, this passage meets me with both challenge and comfort. The challenge is the starkness of the choice. I can't remain undecided forever. Every day, in small ways and large, I am choosing life or choosing death, turning toward the source or drifting away. The comfort is that the word is near. I don't have to climb to heaven or cross the sea. The God who calls me also comes close. The transformation I can't manufacture is offered as a gift.

For those who follow Jesus, this chapter pulses with fulfilment. Paul quotes these very verses in Romans, applying them to the gospel: "The word is near you; it's in your mouth and in your heart," that is, the message concerning Christ. Jesus is the word made near, the command made flesh, the life set before us. In him, the circumcision of the heart that Moses promised becomes reality through the Spirit. In him, the scattered are gathered, the exiled are brought home, the dead are made alive.

And the call remains: choose life. Not once, but daily. Not in theory, but in the concrete decisions that shape who we're becoming. Love God. Listen to that voice. Hold fast. For in Christ, we discover that life isn't something we achieve but someone we receive, the one who is himself the way, the truth, and the life.

Guiding Truth: Choose life today, not as a distant ideal but as a present turning toward the God who is already near, already calling, already offering transformation.

Reflection: In what areas of my life am I drifting rather than choosing, and what would it look like to actively choose life today? Where do I need to trust that God will do in my heart what I can't do for myself?

Prayer: Living God, you set before me life and death, and you call me to choose. Circumcise my heart. Cut away what resists your love. Draw me back from every exile of my own making. Teach me to hold fast to you, for you are my life. Today, I choose you. Amen.

Day 43: Moses Commissions Joshua and Writes the Law

Reading: Deuteronomy 31:1–29

Moses is 120 years old. His eyes are undimmed, his strength unabated, but God has spoken: he won't cross the Jordan. The leader who confronted Pharaoh, who stretched his hand over the sea, who climbed Sinai in fire and cloud, who endured forty years of complaint and rebellion, this leader must now hand over everything to someone else. The work will continue. He won't be there to see it.

This is one of the most poignant transitions in Scripture. Moses gathers the people and speaks with the honesty of someone who has nothing left to protect. "I'm no longer able to lead you," he says. Not because strength has failed, but because God has set a boundary. Leadership has limits. Calling has seasons. Even the greatest servants must learn to release what they have carried.

And yet, in the very breath that acknowledges his ending, Moses points to continuity. "The Lord your God will cross over ahead of you. Joshua will lead you." The emphasis falls not on Joshua's competence but on God's presence. The real leader has always been the one who goes before. Moses was never the source; he was the servant. And the servant can be replaced because the source remains.

Moses commissions Joshua publicly, before all Israel: "Be strong and courageous. Don't be afraid or terrified, for the Lord your God goes with you; God will never leave you nor forsake you." These words aren't pious sentiment. They're survival instructions for a man about to inherit an impossible task. Joshua has watched Moses carry these people. He knows what it costs. And now he hears the only truth that can sustain him: You won't do this alone. The presence that carried Moses will carry you.

Then Moses does something with lasting consequence: he writes down the law and entrusts it to the priests and elders. The word isn't to remain in one person's memory. It's to be read aloud every seven years, at the Festival of Booths, before all Israel, men, women, children, and foreigners. The community must hear it together. Each generation must encounter it afresh. Memory requires repetition. Identity requires rehearsal. Without the regular reading of the word, the people will forget who they are and whose they are.

God then summons Moses and Joshua to the tent of meeting. The pillar of cloud appears. And God speaks words that are devastating in their clarity: "You're going to rest with your ancestors, and these people will soon prostitute themselves to the foreign gods of the land. They'll forsake me and break the covenant I made with them." God knows what will happen. God isn't surprised by human failure. The rebellion to come is already seen, already grieved, already accounted for.

This foreknowledge doesn't lead God to abandon the project. Instead, God commands Moses to write a song, a witness that will remain when obedience fades, a testimony lodged in the memory of the people that will confront them in their unfaithfulness. The music is meant to interpret failure. When disaster comes, the people won't be able to claim ignorance. The song will rise from their own lips and accuse them.

Moses speaks his final warning to the Levites: "I know how rebellious and stiff-necked you are. If you've been rebellious against the Lord while I'm still alive and with you, how much more will you rebel after I die!" There's no illusion here. Moses doesn't pretend the people are better than they are. He's lived with them long enough to know. And yet he doesn't despair. He does what he can: he writes, he teaches, he commissions, he entrusts. The outcome isn't in his hands. Faithfulness is.

Spiritually, this passage speaks to every ending, every transition, every moment when we must release what we have carried and trust others to continue. It confronts the illusion that we're indispensable. It exposes the grief of letting go. And it anchors hope not in the competence of successors but in the faithfulness of the God who goes before.

For those who follow Jesus, this chapter resonates with the pattern of his own ministry. He, too, prepared others to continue. He, too, entrusted the word to fallible disciples. He, too, knew they would fail: Peter's denial, Thomas's doubt, the scattering at Gethsemane. And yet he commissioned them anyway. "I'm with you always, to the end of the age." The promise Moses spoke to Joshua finds its fulfilment in the risen Christ, who goes ahead of us into every land we're called to enter.

The call to be strong and courageous isn't a demand for self-generated confidence. It's an invitation to lean into a presence that won't leave. Our strength is borrowed. Another sustains our courage. And when our own season of leadership ends, as every season must, we can release with grace, knowing that the one who goes before will continue the work we could only begin.

Guiding Truth: Release what you have carried with grace, the God who goes before you will sustain those who come after.

Reflection: What am I holding onto that God may be calling me to entrust to others? Where do I need to hear again the words "be strong and courageous," not as a demand for self-sufficiency but as an invitation to lean into God's presence?

Prayer: Faithful God, you go before me and remain when I am gone. Teach me to release with grace what I've carried. Strengthen those who will continue the work I can't finish. Anchor my courage not in my own competence but in your unfailing presence. You'll never leave or forsake. That's enough. Amen.

Day 44: The Song of Moses, Part I: Faithfulness and Rebellion

Reading: Deuteronomy 32:1–25

Moses becomes a poet. After the laws, the warnings, the blessings, and the curses, he is given one final task: write a song. Not because songs are ornamental but because songs lodge in memory where prose can't reach. Israel will forget the covenant. They'll abandon the law. But the song will remain, rising unbidden from their lips to witness against them and call them back. This is Scripture set to music, truth that outlasts understanding.

The song begins with a summons to creation itself: "Listen, you heavens . . . Hear, you earth." Moses calls the cosmos as a witness. What he's about to sing isn't private or tribal; it's a word that concerns the whole order of things. Heaven and earth will still be standing when Israel's memory fails. They'll testify when human voices grow silent.

Then comes a stunning declaration of God's character: "He's the Rock, his works are perfect, and all his ways are just. A faithful God who does no wrong, upright and just is he." Before any accusation is levelled at Israel, the song establishes the ground on which everything else stands. God isn't arbitrary. God isn't capricious. Whatever judgment follows flows from an utterly reliable character. The Rock doesn't shift. The problem is never with the foundation.

The contrast is immediate and devastating: "They're corrupt and not his children; to their shame they're a warped and crooked

127

generation." The failure is entirely on the human side. The children have acted nothing like their parents. The beloved have become unrecognisable. Moses asks the question that echoes through every generation of unfaithfulness: "Is this the way you repay the Lord, you foolish and unwise people? Is he not your Father, your Creator, who made you and formed you?"

The song then moves into memory. Moses calls the people to remember the ancient days, to ask the elders, to trace the story back to its source. God found Israel in a desert land, in a barren, howling waste. God shielded them, cared for them, and guarded them as the apple of his eye. The imagery is intimate, tender, fierce. An eagle stirring its nest, hovering over its young, catching them on its wings. God carried them. God alone led them. No foreign god was with them.

The land yielded its abundance. Honey from the rock, oil from the flinty crag, curds and milk, the finest wheat, the foaming blood of the grape. Every gift imaginable was lavished on these people. And then, the turn: "Jeshurun grew fat and kicked." The beloved one, satisfied and sleek, abandoned the God who made them and rejected the Rock their Saviour. Prosperity became the doorway to apostasy. Fullness bred forgetfulness. The very gifts meant to draw them toward gratitude pushed them toward self-sufficiency.

They made God jealous with foreign gods, angered him with detestable idols. They sacrificed to demons, to gods they had not known, to new gods that recently appeared. The tragedy isn't simply that they worshipped other gods, but that those gods were nothing, newcomers, impostors, empty projections of human desire. Israel traded the Rock for rubble, the Creator for creatures of their own imagining.

God's response is grief that becomes judgment: "I'll hide my face from them . . . I'll heap calamities on them." The disasters that follow, famine, plague, wild beasts, sword, terror, aren't arbitrary punishments. They're the withdrawal of protection, the natural consequence of severing the relationship that held everything together. When the source of life is rejected, death floods in through every opening.

Spiritually, this passage lays me bare. I recognise the pattern. I've known seasons of abundance and let them dull my gratitude. I've grown fat on blessings and kicked against the hand that gave them. I've chased after gods that are no gods, approval, security, comfort, control, and wondered why life felt hollow. The song isn't ancient history. It's an autobiography.

And yet the song doesn't leave us in despair. It's designed to expose, to wound, to create the kind of honesty that makes return possible. The Rock remains. The foundation has not shifted. Even when we've been warped and crooked, the one who is upright and still stands, still waits, still offers a way back.

For those who follow Jesus, this song finds its most profound resonance at the cross. There, the faithful one bears the consequence of our unfaithfulness. There, God's face is hidden, not from us, but from the Son who becomes our sin. There, the judgment that should've consumed the crooked generation falls on the upright one. And there, the Rock is struck so that living water might flow to all who have wandered, all who have forgotten, all who are ready to come home.

Guiding Truth: Remember who carried you in the wilderness, and let gratitude, not abundance, be the measure of your faithfulness.

Reflection: Where has abundance quietly dulled my gratitude and drawn my heart toward self-sufficiency? What "gods that are no gods" have I been chasing, and what would it mean to return to the Rock?

Prayer: Faithful God, you're the Rock who doesn't shift. Forgive me for the times I've grown fat on your gifts and forgotten your name. Expose the idols I've chased. Restore the gratitude I've lost. Draw me back to yourself, the only foundation that holds. Amen.

Day 45: The Song of Moses, Part II: Judgment and Redemption

Reading: Deuteronomy 32:26–52

The song turns. Having traced Israel's rebellion and God's grieved response, Moses now reveals something unexpected: God restrains judgment. Not because Israel deserves mercy, but because destruction would send the wrong message. The enemies would misunderstand. They'd say, "Our hand has triumphed; the Lord has not done all this." God's reputation among the nations matters. Even in judgment, God is concerned with witness.

This is a strange and humbling logic. Israel is spared, at least in part, not for their own sake but for the sake of God's name. Grace arrives through an unexpected door. The same pride that led to rebellion is now exposed in the enemies who would claim credit for Israel's downfall. God won't allow the arrogant to write the final interpretation of history.

The song then turns its gaze on the nations themselves. They're a people without sense, without discernment. If they were wise, they'd understand their own end. They'd ask the obvious question: How could one enemy chase a thousand, unless the Rock had sold them, unless the Lord had given them up? Israel's defeats aren't evidence of weak gods but of a strong God disciplining his own. The nations, in their blindness, can't see that their victories are borrowed, temporary, permitted.

And then comes the pivot that changes everything: "The Lord will vindicate his people and relent concerning his servants when he sees their strength is gone, and no one is left." God waits for the bottom. God watches until self-sufficiency is exhausted, until every alternative has failed, until the people finally recognise that the idols they chased can't save. "Where are their gods, the rock they took refuge in?" The question is clarifying. Only when the false refuges collapse can the true Rock be seen again.

God's declaration rises with thunder: "See now that I myself am he! There's no god besides me. I put to death, and I bring to life, I have wounded, and I'll heal, and no one can deliver out of my hand." This is the announcement that the one who judged is also the one who restores. The hand that wounded is the hand that heals. There's no other saviour to seek. The search is over. The Rock stands alone.

The song ends with a call to rejoice, not despite judgment but through it. "Rejoice, you nations, with his people, for he'll avenge the blood of his servants; he'll take vengeance on his enemies and make atonement for his land and people." Atonement. The word appears here, at the song's close, like a door cracking open. Judgment isn't the end. Cleansing is coming. The land and the people will be restored.

Moses speaks every word of this song in the hearing of the people. Then God summons him to Mount Nebo. He'll see the land from a distance, the land he has journeyed toward for forty years, but he won't enter. The reason is named: "Because you broke faith with me . . . because you didn't uphold my holiness." Even Moses bears consequences. Even the most excellent servant isn't exempt. The holiness of God isn't negotiable, not even for those who have been faithful in so much else.

And yet the tone isn't bitter. Moses isn't cast off; he is gathered. He'll die on the mountain, seeing the promise even if he can't touch it. There's grief here, but also completion. The work is done. The song is sung. The people have been warned and blessed. What remains is rest.

Spiritually, this passage holds together truths I struggle to reconcile. God judges and God heals. God wounds and God restores. The same hand does both. I want a God who only comforts, but the song insists that comfort without truth is no comfort at all. The Rock is faithful precisely because the Rock doesn't pretend. Consequences are real. And so is mercy.

For those who follow Jesus, this song's ending reverberates with gospel. The atonement Moses glimpsed is accomplished at Calvary. The one who puts to death and brings to life does both in a single act, dying and rising, wounded and healing, absorbing judgment and offering restoration. The nations are called to rejoice with God's people because the blessing of Abraham has spilled over to the whole world. The Rock, who was struck, now pours out living water for all who thirst.

And like Moses, we may not see every promise fulfilled in our lifetime. We may climb our own Nebo and glimpse from a distance what we won't touch. But the song we have sung, the witness we have borne, the faithfulness we have practised, these aren't lost. They're gathered into a story larger than our own, carried forward by the God who brings to life what has died.

Guiding Truth: Trust the God who wounds and heals, judgment and mercy flow from the same faithful hand.

Reflection: Where have I resisted God's discipline, wanting comfort without truth? What false refuges need to collapse before I can see the Rock clearly again?

Prayer: God of judgment and mercy, I trust that your wounding leads to healing. Expose the false refuges I have built. Bring me to the end of my self-sufficiency so I can see you clearly. You alone put to death and bring to life. You alone are my Rock. Amen.

Day 46: Moses Blesses the Tribes, Part I

Reading: Deuteronomy 33:1–17

Moses is called "the man of God." It's one of the few times Scripture uses this title, and it appears here, at the end, as a kind of summary. Whatever else Moses was, leader, lawgiver, prophet, intercessor, he was, above all, someone who belonged to God and through whom God spoke. Now, in his final act, he does what dying parents have always done: he blesses his children. Tribe by tribe, he speaks words of destiny, identity, and hope over the people he has carried for forty years.

The blessing begins not with the tribes but with God. Moses recalls the theophany at Sinai: the Lord coming from Sinai, dawning over Seir, shining forth from Mount Paran, arriving with myriads of holy ones, lightning flashing from his right hand. The imagery is overwhelming: fire, mountain, armies of heaven. Before any tribe is named, Moses anchors everything in the God who appeared, who spoke, who gave the law, and who loved the people. Blessing flows from encounter. Identity is rooted in revelation.

"Surely it's you who love the people; all the holy ones are in your hand." This is the theological foundation beneath every tribal blessing. God's love isn't sentiment; it's action, protection, and presence. The holy ones, whether angels or Israel itself, are held. Nothing can snatch them away. Whatever specific words follow for each tribe, they rest on this bedrock: you are loved, you are held, you belong to the one who came in fire and gave the law as inheritance.

The blessing of Reuben is brief and poignant: "Let Reuben live and not die, nor his people be few." There's no lavish promise here, only survival. Reuben, the firstborn who forfeited his birthright, receives a modest word, enough to continue, sufficient to endure. Sometimes blessing isn't abundance but persistence. Sometimes the grace we need is to keep going.

Judah's blessing is a cry for help and victory: "Hear, Lord, the cry of Judah; bring him to his people. With his own hands, he defends his cause. Oh, be his help against his foes!" Judah will carry the weight of leadership, the burden of battle. Moses prays not for ease but for divine assistance in the struggle. The blessing acknowledges that Judah will fight, and asks that God fight alongside.

Levi receives one of the longest blessings. This is the priestly tribe, set apart for teaching, intercession, and sacrifice. Moses recalls the testing at Massah and Meribah, where Levi proved faithful when others faltered. The Levites "watched over your word and guarded your covenant." They set aside family loyalty for the sake of divine loyalty, a costly, painful, necessary choice. And because of that fidelity, they're entrusted with the Thummim and Urim, with teaching the law, with offering incense and sacrifice. Blessing here is vocation. It's the privilege of proximity to God, purchased through painful obedience.

Benjamin is called "the beloved of the Lord," who rests secure, shielded all day long, dwelling between God's shoulders. The imagery is tender, a child carried, protected, held close. Benjamin's portion will be near the temple mount, close to the place where God's presence dwells. Some tribes are blessed with strength; Benjamin is blessed with nearness. Both are gifts.

Joseph receives the most elaborate blessing, cascading with images of abundance: the precious dew from heaven, the deep waters beneath, the best gifts of sun and moon, the choicest fruits of ancient mountains, the favour of the one who dwelt in the burning bush. Joseph's descendants, Ephraim and Manasseh, will be numerous and powerful, goring the nations like a wild ox. The blessing is extravagant, almost excessive, a pouring out of fruitfulness on the one whose story was already marked by suffering, redeemed.

Spiritually, these blessings reveal something about how God sees. Each tribe is known. Each receives a word fitted to its history, its calling, its need. There's no generic blessing here, no one-size-fits-all formula. Reuben needs survival; Judah needs strength; Levi needs vocation; Benjamin needs tenderness; Joseph needs abundance. God's blessing is personal, particular, attentive to who we actually are.

For those who follow Jesus, this passage anticipates the way Christ knows and blesses his own. He calls each by name. He speaks specific words of commission, comfort, and calling. He sees what we have endured, what we're capable of, what we need to flourish. The blessing isn't an impersonal favour but an intimate knowledge. And the God who came in fire at Sinai now comes in flesh at Bethlehem, still loving the people, still holding the holy ones, still speaking words of life over those who belong to him.

To receive a blessing is to be seen, named, and sent. It's good to hear a word that tells you who you are and whose you are. Moses' final gift to Israel is this: You aren't anonymous. You are known. And the God who knows you also blesses you with precisely what you need.

Guiding Truth: Receive the blessing fitted to your story. God sees who you are and speaks the particular word you need.

Reflection: What blessing do I most need right now, survival, strength, vocation, tenderness, or abundance? How does knowing that God's blessing is personal and particular change how I receive it?

Prayer: God who loves your people and holds them in your hand, speak the blessing I need. You know my story, my struggles, my calling. Meet me with the particular word that fits who I am. Let your blessing name me, steady me, and send me into the life you have prepared. Amen.

Day 47: Moses Blesses the Tribes, Part II

Reading: Deuteronomy 33:18–29

Moses continues blessing the tribes, and each word carries the weight of finality. These aren't predictions to be analysed but benedictions to be received. The dying prophet speaks life over his people, naming their gifts, their callings, their futures. And woven through the particular blessings is a vision of God that'll sustain Israel long after Moses is gone.

Zebulun and Issachar are blessed together: "Rejoice, Zebulun, in your going out, and you, Issachar, in your tents." One tribe ventures forth; the other remains home. One is called to movement; the other to stability. Both are blessed. The life of faith doesn't require a single posture. Some are sent out to engage the world; others are called to anchor the community. Zebulun will draw wealth from the seas; Issachar will feast on the treasures of the sand. Each has a place. Each contributes. The body needs both travellers and tent-dwellers.

Gad is blessed as a lion, settling in the best land, carrying out God's righteous will. "He chose the best land for himself; the leader's portion was kept for him." There is no rebuke here for Gad's earlier request to settle east of the Jordan. What might've seemed like self-interest is reframed as destiny. Sometimes what looks like grasping is actually receiving what was always meant to be. Gad fought for the other tribes before claiming rest. The blessing honours both the fighting and the settling.

Dan is a "lion's cub, springing out of Bashan", fierce, sudden, powerful. The image is brief but vivid. Dan will be small but formidable, a tribe whose strength exceeds its size. Not every blessing is about abundance. Some are about intensity, about concentrated power, about being exactly what is needed in the moment of crisis.

Naphtali receives one of the most beautiful blessings: "Abounding with the favour of the Lord and full of his blessing, possess the south and the west." Favour and fullness. Possession and peace. Naphtali's territory will include the Sea of Galilee, where centuries later another blessing will be spoken, where Jesus will call fishermen, teach multitudes, and multiply loaves. The land Moses blesses will become the stage for gospel.

Asher is blessed with strength and security: "Most blessed of sons is Asher; let him be favoured by his brothers, and let him bathe his feet in oil. The bolts of your gates will be iron and bronze, and your strength will equal your days." Oil for abundance, iron for protection, strength matched to need. Asher won't face more than it can bear. The blessing promises proportionality, resources sufficient for the journey, defences adequate for the threat, energy lasting as long as the task requires.

Then Moses lifts his eyes beyond the tribes to the God who rides across the heavens, who comes to help on the clouds. "There is no one like the God of Jeshurun, who rides across the heavens to help you and on the clouds in his majesty." The particular blessings find their source in this universal truth: the God of Israel is incomparable. No rival. No equal. The one who blesses is also the one who protects, who carries, who fights.

"The eternal God is your dwelling place, and underneath are the everlasting arms." This is perhaps the most beloved line in all of Deuteronomy. Whatever the tribes will face, war, famine, exile, loss, underneath them, always, are arms that don't tire, don't fail, don't let go. The blessing isn't immunity from suffering but presence within it. The arms are everlasting. They were there before Israel existed. They'll remain when Israel has forgotten itself. The foundation holds.

The chapter closes with a triumphant declaration: "Blessed are you, Israel! Who is like you, a people saved by the Lord? He is your shield and helper and your glorious sword. Your enemies will cower before you, and you will tread on their heights." The blessing isn't wishful thinking. It's reality declared in advance. Israel is already saved. The victory is already won. What remains is to live into what has been spoken.

Spiritually, this passage wraps around me like the arms it describes. I need to hear that there is no one like God, that the eternal arms are underneath, that my strength will equal my days. I need to know that whether I am a Zebulun going out or an Issachar staying home, I am blessed. The particular shape of my calling doesn't determine the depth of my blessing. What matters is the God who speaks it.

For those who follow Jesus, these final blessings resonate with the benedictions he speaks over his own. "Peace I leave with you; my peace I give you." "I am with you always, to the end of the age." The everlasting arms have taken on flesh. The God who rides across the heavens has walked the dusty roads of Galilee. The shield, helper, and glorious sword has become the Lamb who was slain. And still the promise holds: underneath are the everlasting arms.

Guiding Truth: Rest in the everlasting arms beneath you, your strength will equal your days, and the God who blesses you will never let go.

Reflection: Where do I need to trust that the everlasting arms are underneath me right now? How does knowing that my strength will equal my days change how I face what lies ahead?

Prayer: Eternal God, you are my dwelling place. When I fall, your arms catch me. When I tire, your strength sustains me. Teach me to rest in the blessing you have spoken over my life. There is no one like you. Ride across the heavens to help me, and hold me until the end. Amen.

Day 48: Moses' Final Vision from Mount Nebo

Reading: Deuteronomy 34:1–4

Moses climbs. One hundred and twenty years old, eyes undimmed, strength unabated, he ascends Mount Nebo to the peak of Pisgah. Below him stretches the Jordan Valley. Beyond it lies everything he has journeyed toward for forty years. And God shows him the land, all of it. Gilead to Dan in the north. Naphtali, Ephraim, Manasseh, Judah stretching to the Mediterranean. The Negev in the south. The plain of Jericho, city of palms, shimmering in the distance. Moses sees it all.

This isn't natural sight. No human eye could take in such a panorama from a single peak. God is giving Moses a vision, a gift beyond geography. The land that was promised to Abraham, Isaac, and Jacob is spread before him like a scroll unrolled. "I have let you see it with your eyes," God says, "but you won't cross over into it." The promise is real. The land is real. Moses won't touch it.

There is grief here, but not bitterness. Moses has known for some time that this would be his end. The striking of the rock, the moment of faithlessness at Meribah, sealed his fate. He pleaded with God to relent, and God said no. Now he stands on the mountain, receiving what he can, sight without possession, vision without arrival. It's both gift and limit, grace and consequence held together in a single moment.

What must it have felt like? To see Jericho's walls in the distance, knowing Joshua would bring them down. To see the hills of Judah, knowing David would one day reign there. To see the Jordan, knowing his feet would never feel its water. Moses had carried this people through their worst rebellions, had interceded when God was ready to destroy them, had climbed Sinai in fire and descended with glory on his face. And now, at the end, he is given a glimpse but not an entrance.

This is the mystery of faithful service. We plant seeds we won't harvest. We begin work others will finish. We catch visions of futures we won't inhabit. Moses' life was not a failure because he did not enter the land. His life was faithful because he climbed the mountain anyway, received the vision with gratitude, and trusted that the God who showed him the land would bring his people into it.

Spiritually, this passage confronts me with the limits of my own story. I want to see the completion of what I begin. I want to arrive, not just journey. I want the satisfaction of crossing over, not the ache of seeing from a distance. But Moses teaches me that faithfulness isn't measured by arrival. It's measured by obedience, by trust, by the willingness to climb even when the summit offers only a view of what will never be mine.

There is also comfort here. God doesn't leave Moses in ignorance. The vision is a kindness. Moses doesn't die wondering what might've been. He sees. He knows. The promise is true. The land is good. His people will flourish there. The seeing is itself a form of participation, a communion with the future even without physical presence. God honours Moses with sight because sight is a way of blessing.

For those who follow Jesus, this mountaintop moment echoes forward. Centuries later, on another mountain, Moses will appear, this time standing with Elijah and Jesus, talking about the "exodus" Jesus is about to accomplish in Jerusalem. The one who could not enter Canaan now stands on the soil of the promised land, transfigured in glory. What was denied in death is granted in resurrection. The story doesn't end on Nebo. It ends in fulfilment beyond anything Moses could have imagined.

And for us, the same hope holds. We won't see the completion of every promise in this life. We'll climb mountains and glimpse futures we can't touch. But the God who showed Moses the land is the God who raised Jesus from the dead. The visions we're given aren't cruel teases; they're foretastes of a fulfilment that death itself can't prevent. What we see from our Nebo, we'll one day walk in, transformed, completed, home.

Guiding Truth: Trust the vision God gives you, even when you can't cross over, faithfulness isn't measured by arrival but by obedience to the end.

Reflection: What "promised land" am I longing to enter that I may only see from a distance in this life? How does Moses' example reshape my understanding of what it means to be faithful even without arriving?

Prayer: God of promise, you show me more than I can hold. Teach me to receive the vision with gratitude, even when I can't cross over. Free me from measuring faithfulness by arrival. Give me grace to climb the mountain, see the land, and trust that what you have promised will come to pass, if not through me, then through those who follow. Amen.

Day 49: The Death of Moses and the Transition to Joshua

Reading: Deuteronomy 34:5–8

"And Moses the servant of the Lord died there in Moab, as the Lord had said." The sentence is plain, almost abrupt. No drama, no prolonged farewell, no final speech. Moses simply dies. After the plagues and the sea, the manna and the quail, the thunder of Sinai and the glow of his own face, the rebellions and intercessions, the songs and blessings: after all of it, Moses dies. The greatest prophet Israel would ever know breathes his last on a mountain, alone with God.

But the following line is extraordinary: "He buried him in Moab, in the valley opposite Beth Peor, but to this day no one knows where his grave is." God buries Moses. Not Aaron, not Joshua, not the elders. God. The one who called him from the burning bush now lays him to rest. The intimacy is staggering. Moses, who spoke with God face to face, is now carried by those same hands into the earth. The master, the child by the parent, the friend by the friend, buries the servant.

The hidden grave is significant. Israel won't be able to build a shrine to Moses' bones. There will be no pilgrimages to his tomb, no temptation to venerate the man instead of the God he served. Moses pointed beyond himself his entire life; even in death, he refuses to become an idol. The hiddenness protects both his legacy and Israel's faith. The focus must remain on the living God, not the departed prophet.

"Moses was a hundred and twenty years old when he died, yet his eyes weren't weak nor his strength gone." This isn't natural. At 120, eyes dim and bodies fail. But Moses dies whole, not from decay but by divine appointment. His death isn't a defeat; it's a completion. The work is done. The words are spoken. The blessing is given. There's nothing left unfinished, nothing left unsaid. Moses dies full, not empty.

"The Israelites grieved for Moses in the plains of Moab thirty days, until the time of weeping and mourning was over." Thirty days. A whole month of tears. The people who had so often grumbled against Moses now weep for him. The one they accused of leading them out to die is now mourned as irreplaceable. Grief has a way of clarifying what we failed to see when someone was still with us. Israel finally understands what they had and what they have lost.

But the mourning has a limit. Thirty days, and then it ends. Grief is honoured, but grief isn't permanent. There is a river to cross, a land to enter, a future to embrace. Joshua waits. The people must move. Mourning that never ends becomes paralysis. The God who allowed time for tears now calls for movement. Honouring the dead means living fully, not stopping forever.

Spiritually, this passage holds together realities I often want to keep separate: the finality of death and the tenderness of God, the irreplaceability of a leader and the necessity of transition, the depth of grief and the call to continue. Moses' death teaches me that even the most extraordinary lives end, that even the most faithful servants are buried, and that the story goes on because the God of the story doesn't die.

There is also profound comfort here. If God buries Moses, then death isn't abandonment. The hands that guided through the wilderness guide through the valley of shadow. The presence that never leaves in life doesn't go in death. Moses dies "as the Lord had said," not as tragedy but as fulfilment. Even death, for those who belong to God, is held within the purposes of grace.

For those who follow Jesus, this passage anticipates a greater death and a greater burial. Jesus, too, will die on a hill, outside the camp, carrying the weight of a people's rebellion. He, too, will be buried, but his grave won't remain hidden. It'll be empty. The God who buried Moses will raise the Son. And because of that resurrection, every death held in Christ becomes not an ending but a passage, not a defeat but a doorway.

Moses' death is real. The grief is real. The transition is necessary. But underneath it all, the everlasting arms still hold. The God who buried his servant will also raise the dead. The story continues because the Storyteller lives.

Guiding Truth: Trust that the God who holds you in life will carry you through death and that the story continues because the Storyteller lives.

Reflection: How do I hold together the reality of grief and the call to continue living? What does it mean to trust that God's hands will carry me even through death?

Prayer: Faithful God, you buried your servant Moses with your own hands. Hold me in life and carry me through death. When grief overwhelms, give me space to mourn. When mourning ends, please give me the courage to move. Teach me that the story continues because you live, and my life is held in yours. Amen.

Day 50: Remembering the Prophet and the Promise Beyond

Reading: Deuteronomy 34:9–12

The book of Deuteronomy closes with a transfer and a tribute. Joshua, filled with the spirit of wisdom because Moses had laid hands on him, steps into leadership. The people listen to him. The work continues. The torch has been passed. What Moses began, Joshua will carry forward. The story doesn't end with Moses' death; it turns a page.

But before the page turns, the narrator pauses to honour what has been. "Since then, no prophet has risen in Israel like Moses, whom the Lord knew face to face." This is the highest tribute Scripture offers to any human being. Face to face. Not through dreams or visions, not through angels or riddles, but directly, personally, intimately. Moses knew God, and God knew Moses, with a closeness that set him apart from every prophet who would follow.

The signs and wonders are named: everything Moses did in Egypt, the mighty power, the wondrous deeds performed before all Israel. The plagues that broke Pharaoh's grip. The sea that parted. The mountain that burned. The water from the rock. The manna that fell. The serpents that healed. Moses was not merely a teacher of laws; he was a channel of divine power, a man through whom the impossible became visible.

And yet, for all his greatness, Moses pointed beyond himself. The very book that celebrates him also records his failure at Meribah, his exclusion from the land, and his humanity. Moses isn't deified. He is honoured as the greatest of prophets and buried in an unmarked grave. The tension is deliberate. Israel isn't to worship Moses; Israel is to remember him as a sign of what God can do through a faithful, flawed human being.

The phrase "no prophet has risen in Israel like Moses" is both a tribute and an anticipation. It closes one chapter while leaving another open. If no prophet like Moses has yet arisen, might one still come? Deuteronomy 18 promised exactly that: "The Lord your God will raise up for you a prophet like me from among your own people." The ending of Deuteronomy isn't merely retrospective; it's expectant. Israel is meant to watch, to wait, to hope for the one who will surpass even Moses.

Joshua is faithful, but he isn't that prophet. The judges will come and go. Kings will rise and fall. Prophets will thunder and weep. But none will know God face to face as Moses did. The longing remains. The promise is unfulfilled. Deuteronomy ends with Israel looking backward in gratitude and forward in hope.

Spiritually, this passage invites me to hold memory and hope together. I'm shaped by those who have gone before, the teachers, mentors, and saints who carried me when I could not walk. I honour their faithfulness. I grieve their absence. But I don't stop there. The God who worked through them is still working. The promise they embodied is still unfolding. The story they began isn't finished.

For those who follow Jesus, this closing passage bursts into fulfilment. The prophet like Moses has come. The one who knows God face to face, not as a servant in the house, but as the Son over it, has appeared. Jesus is greater than Moses. He doesn't merely deliver from Egypt; he delivers from sin and death. He doesn't simply part the sea; he walks on it. He doesn't merely give the law; he fulfils it. He doesn't die on a mountain, excluded from the promise; he dies on a cross, opening the promise to the whole world.

And yet, like Israel at the end of Deuteronomy, we too live between memory and hope. We remember what Christ has done. We anticipate what he will complete. We honour the saints who have gone before while pressing forward toward the prize. The book closes, but the story continues. The prophet has come, and the prophet will come again. Until then, we walk by faith, shaped by the past, leaning into the future, held by the God who knew Moses face to face and now, through Christ, invites us into that same intimacy.

Deuteronomy ends where all faithful lives end: with work completed, blessing spoken, and the future entrusted to God. Moses rests. Joshua leads. Israel crosses. And the God who was faithful to Abraham, Isaac, and Jacob remains faithful still, calling, forming, redeeming, until every promise finds its "yes" in Christ.

Guiding Truth: Honour those who have gone before, but fix your eyes on the one who fulfils every promise, the prophet greater than Moses has come, and he is coming again.

Reflection: Who are the "Moses figures" in my life whose faithfulness has shaped me, and how do I honour their legacy while pressing forward? How does knowing that Jesus is the fulfillment of Deuteronomy's hope change how I live between memory and anticipation?

Prayer: Faithful God, thank you for Moses and for all who have pointed me toward you. Thank you even more for Jesus, the prophet greater than Moses, who knows you face to face and brings me into that same intimacy. Help me honour the past while pressing toward the future you are preparing. Until every promise is fulfilled, keep me faithful. Amen.

Appendix 1: Would You Help?

Writing a book takes immense effort. It's a sustained labor of love over months, even years. Every page carries hours of thought, prayer, revision, and hope. And while the writing may be solitary, the life of a book is communal. That's where you come in. If this book has meant something to you, I'd be deeply grateful if you could help it find its way into more hands and hearts.

There are two simple but powerful ways you can do that.

First, consider leaving a short review on Amazon (and Goodreads would be wonderful too). Even just a few sentences can help others discover the book, as reviews significantly influence how books are recommended and shared online. You can do that by visiting Amazon or searching for this book and writing a review. Even a short note helps people find the book.

Second, if the book has stirred something in you, would you share it with others: friends, groups, churches, or anyone who might benefit from its message?

Your support helps keep this work going, and it means more than I can say. Thank you for being part of this journey.

Find this book on these pages:

1. Amazon:

https://www.amazon.com.au/stores/author/B008NI4ORQ

2. Goodreads:

https://www.goodreads.com/author/show/20347171.Graham_Joseph _Hill

3. Author Website:

https://grahamjosephhill.com/books/

Appendix 2: About Me

Graham Joseph Hill (OAM, PhD) is an Adjunct Research Fellow and Associate Professor at Charles Sturt University, and one of Australia's most prolific and awarded Christian authors. He's written more than thirty books, including *Salt, Light, and a City*, which was named Jesus Creed's 2012 Book of the Year (church category); *Healing Our Broken Humanity* (with Grace Ji-Sun Kim), named Outreach Magazine's 2019 Resource of the Year (culture category); and *World Christianity*, shortlisted for the 2025 Australian Christian Book of the Year. In 2024, Graham was awarded the Medal of the Order of Australia (OAM) for his service to theological education. He lives in Sydney with his wife, Shyn.

Author and Ministry Websites

GrahamJosephHill.com
GrahamJosephHill.Substack.com
youtube.com/@GrahamJosephHill_Author
Linktr.ee/dailydevotions
facebook.com/grahamjosephhill/
instagram.com/grahamjosephhill/
amazon.com.au/stores/author/B008NI4ORQ
goodreads.com/author/show/20347171.Graham_Joseph_Hill

Books

See all my books at GrahamJosephHill.com/books

Appendix 3: Connect With Me

I'd love to stay connected with you. You can sign up to my Substack, Spirituality and Society with Hilly, where I share new writing, spiritual reflections, and updates on future books. Please find me on Substack: https://grahamjosephhill.substack.com

You can also find my books on my website:
https://grahamjosephhill.com/books

You can also connect with me through my Facebook author page:
https://www.facebook.com/GrahamJosephHill/